# North American
# RAILYARDS

Michael Rhodes

MBI

First published in 2003 by MBI Publishing Company, Galtier Plaza, Suite 200, 380 Jackson Street, St. Paul, MN 55101-3885 USA

MBI titles are also available at discounts in bulk quantity for industrial or sales-promotional use. For details write to Special Sales Manager at Motorbooks International Wholesalers & Distributors, Galtier Plaza, Suite 200, 380 Jackson Street, St. Paul, MN 55101-3885 USA.

Library of Congress Cataloging-in-Publication Data Available

ISBN 0-7603-1578-7

**Front Cover:** The sun has just set on Yermo Yard in March 1993. This view taken from the west clearly shows the facility's layout. To the south are 18 short classification tracks, with a pair of four-axle locomotives pulling cars in the far right. The eight longer roads used for arrivals and departures and two UP manifests also can be seen in the far right. Behind these manifests are the run-through tracks used for COFC and unit trains. The eagle-eyed may just be able to make out a unit coal train leaving to the east about a mile away, looking like a black snake on the horizon.

**Endpapers:** This view from the Alyth Yard hump tower in Calgary, Alberta, was taken in April 1998, and shows a boxcar rolling into one of six classification fans, each made up of eight tracks.

**Frontis:** A solitary grain car rolls down the eastbound hump at Bailey Yard in North Platte, Nebraska, and into one of 64 classification tracks for traffic. It is just being arrested by one of two primary retarders and eventually will be slowed to less than 4 miles per hour to avoid damaging itself and the other cars in the bowl.

**Title Page:** Dawn at Osborn Yard in Louisville, Kentucky, May 1998. The classification bowl is quiet as workers change shifts in the hump tower. The departure tracks lie to the right and left of the main bowl.

**Back Cover Top:** Carload country. The bowl at Seattle's Pasco Yard shows no sign of intermodal or high-capacity cars. Even in 1996, when this view was taken, it looks much as it would have when it opened in 1955.

**Back Cover Bottom:** Somehow, Bill Clinton had to be from Little Rock.

Edited by Dennis Pernu
Designed by Mandy Iverson

Printed in China

The list of people who have helped with this book over a 14-year period is enormous. It's not possible to list them all, but I would particularly like to thank Bob Del Grosso, William W. Kratville, Dave Norris, John Bennet, Mike Walker, Harry Ladd, Carl Ardrey, Lynn Burshtin, Leslie Dean, Woodrow M. Cunningham, William H. Demsey, and the hundreds of yardmasters, switchers, and rail workers who have let me photograph them at work and visit their yards.

My thanks also go to MBI Publishing Company, and also to a host of rail employees and railfans who have both knowingly and unknowingly helped with this book. I have been amazed at the hospitality and kindness of railway employees. I have been invited to join the local freemasons in one control tower, have been fed sizzling hamburgers at a railroad barbecue at another yard, and have been made welcome almost everywhere. Thanks also to all the yardmasters who have given me coffee and spared me their time to explain the operations of their own yards so patiently.

To anyone I have omitted, I extend my apologies and my gratitude for your help. Needless to say, any errors or omissions are my own.

This employee at Oak Island Yard in Newark, New Jersey, was just one of the hundreds of rail workers who gave me their time during the 14 years it took me to compile this book.

# INTRODUCTION

The humble classification yard has attracted little attention in the railway press, and no publication has ever documented the life and times of these important railway facilities. The classification yard is the focus of carload freight operations on any railroad. This is nowhere more evident than in the United States, where 90 percent of railroad traffic is freight. To the freight railroad, a major classification yard is like the grand terminus of the more glamorous passenger side of operations.

Just like the ornate Union termini before them, the classification yard is becoming an endangered species for several reasons: mergers and consolidations that have caused a decline in railroad traffic and the elimination of duplicate functions; a decline in carload traffic, paralleled by rapid expansion in intermodal services; and the paving of much of the land needed for the intermodal network, in order to allow parking for road trailers.

A 1993 report by Deco Ltd. (the largest supplier of mechanical retarders) revealed that there were 147 hump classification yards in North America in 1970. By 1993, just 72 were left. However, those in the railyard business predicted that by 1999 there would be only 46. This prophecy has proven pessimistic. A survey conducted as this book closed for press revealed that more than 60 hump classification yards remain in active service in the United States and Canada.

The origins of the hump or summit yard date back to the 1880s in Europe. As did France and Germany, the British used gravity for classification in their Liverpool "grid-iron," which was fully operational in the late 1880s. The first gravity-assisted classification yard in the United States was probably built in 1890 at Honey Pot, on the Sunbury Division of the Pennsylvania Railroad. By the first decade of the 1900s, several much larger and more ambitious schemes had been completed at famous locations such as Enola, Pennsylvania, and Clearing, in Chicago, and the proliferation of hump yards began.

The size of such facilities often means that they are located out of town and away from centers of population. Many big cities have only small classification yards, because the remarshaling of freight cars is often undertaken at focal points on a rail system, perhaps where two or more major routes meet.

Sometimes, information about classification yards is hard to come by, and even their location can be a mystery to many interested in railroads. This book aims to provide the reader with a listing of major classification yards in the United States and Canada. I have attempted to present a clear idea of their layout and operations, and also how best to find the various yards and observe railway action in their vicinity.

Finding the various yards can be a challenge. The reader is advised to refer to either Rand McNally street maps if the yard is in a sizable city or to DeLorme atlases if the yard is out in the countryside. It can be difficult to obtain the appropriate street maps unless one is actually *in* the relevant area. The best way is often to stop at a gas station near or in town, where the relevant maps are invariably for sale. Both Rand McNally maps (www.randmcnally.com) and DeLorme topographic atlases (www.delorme.com) are available for sale online.

This book had its origins in a delayed 1989 flight to Minneapolis, Minnesota. As the Northwest Airlines 747 circled the city in a holding "stack," I looked down and saw the sprawling tracks of Northtown Yard, stretched out for several miles to the north of town. Around this time, the last of my native Britain's classification yards had closed for traffic as United Kingdom railroads moved to predominantly unit trains and intermodal services. From over 40 large hump yards, the U.K. now had none.

After my plane landed, I was pleased to persuade my host at the Mayo Clinic in Rochester, Minnesota, that a Saturday in Minneapolis would be a good idea. Even though I had been a resident of Rochester in the 1960s and was therefore used to American life, I was completely lost when it came to finding Northtown. U.S. maps do not give much prominence to railroads and often fail to show them at all. Furthermore, asking a member of the general public for directions to a "freight yard" tends to elicit bemused stares rather than concise instructions. It is almost as if these vast facilities, often several miles long, are invisible.

After several hours of driving around the city, we finally found Northtown and spent an enjoyable hour in the tower. I am sure the yardmaster thought we were crazy but harmless. He told us there was another hump yard in the Twin Cities at Pig's Eye, but despite our best efforts, we never found it.

When I returned to the United Kingdom, I started writing to the railroads and various historical societies, to find out how many of these massive hump yards were left in North America and where they were. I have listed some sources of help in the acknowledgments section, but one thing became evident: nobody had a clear overview of the country's railyards.

Not only that, but some yards, such as North Platte, were mentioned by everybody with whom I corresponded, while others were mentioned just occasionally, with question marks next to them because their operational status was unknown. *TRAINS Magazine* was an excellent source of information, and material from several older books provided an excellent historical profile of the yards in North America. In the end, though, it became clear that visiting the yards for myself was the only way to get a clear picture of their scale and operations, even though one or two of the visits were disasters.

For example, Taylor Yard in Los Angeles was listed as a major Southern Pacific yard in the excellent *Train Watcher's Guide to North American Railroads*, published in 1993. However, when I visited the site in March 1993, I found only a vast expanse of rubble. The yard had been completely demolished some time previous. A similar site greeted me at Toledo's Walbridge Yard. Other yards posed a different problem; for example, the facilities at Yermo and Hinkle were almost impossible to track down without local knowledge, because no towns bear those names.

Yet more problems arose in large cities because the street plans often omitted rail lines. I was left looking for gaps in the street pattern into which a large yard might fit. One particularly difficult yard to track down was Boyles Yard, in suburban Birmingham, Alabama, which took more than five hours of driving to locate.

Thus, what started as idle curiosity in 1989 became a long-term project to document and visit as many of the American freight yards as possible; the result is this book. Updated information on yards that have been rebuilt, downsized, or changed significantly since I visited them has also been included.

—Michael Rhodes
Norwich, England 2003

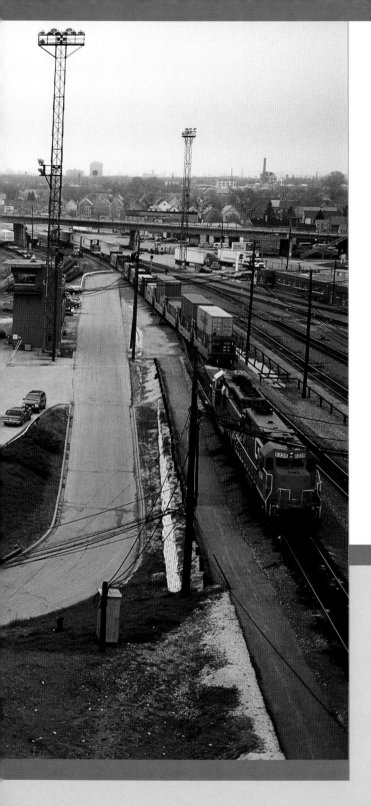

The modern-day Burlington Northern Santa Fe (BNSF) is one of the big two western railroads, and in 2002 it still had eight active hump yards. Two of these were equipped with state-of-the-art Dowty retarders (Hobson Yard in Lincoln and Argentine Yard in Kansas City), while the other six used the more traditional rail-brake technology.

In 1970, four independent railroads merged to form the Burlington Northern (BN). Several major construction projects helped consolidate freight-switching in big cities. The largest of these projects was the 1970s construction of the Northtown Yard.

When BN merged with the Santa Fe in the mid-1990s, the tracks owned by BNSF linked nearly 20 hump yards, but this involved significant duplication of services, which the merger has since consolidated. The Santa Fe had possessed large hump yards at only three locations and was known more for its intermodal traffic than for carload freight. Since the merger, the BNSF has closed the Cicero Yard in Chicago, converting the site into a massive intermodal facility. BNSF has also expanded the Galesburg Yard to act as the eastern focal point for all carload traffic and has concentrated all switching in Kansas City on a totally rebuilt Argentine Yard.

A panorama of the hump bowl at Cicero in May 1995 shows the yard still busy with carload traffic. Through the low clouds and gloom, the skyscrapers of downtown Chicago are just visible 7 or 8 miles away. The long, low bridge across the 42 classification tracks is Laramie Street. Beyond it, about a mile farther away, is a metal girder structure, Austin Boulevard.

The hump at Cicero Yard finally closed in 1997, at the end of October. This was quite a transformation for a yard that had been one of the Burlington Northern's—and one of Chicago's—busiest in 1970, when the railroad was formed. The 250-acre site stretches 2.3 miles, and its 17 reception tracks led to a 42-track classification bowl that handled 3,000 cars each day.

By 1987, the carload traffic had decreased in volume, but there were still daily manifest departures to Galesburg, Seattle, Houston, Kansas City, Denver, Northtown, and Laurel, Montana. This volume translated into a throughput of 33,000 cars per month over the hump. More than 20 switch jobs were done each day in managing the yard and serving local industry.

However, drastic changes had occurred in the nearly two decades since BN had been created. In 1988, the terminal at Cicero was already handling 1,500 trailer lifts each day. The gradual conversion to an intermodal trailers-on-flatcars (TOFC) and containers-on-flatcars (COFC) terminal was evident by the mid-1980s and was to continue until the hump closed in 1997. A visit in 1995 revealed that only 400 cars each day were classified over the hump.

By 1996, BNSF's $8-million investment in increased intermodal facilities at both Corwith and Cicero was the final death knell for the hump. The Chicago, Burlington & Quincy (CB&Q) facility was turned over entirely to container freight. Carload classification was relocated to Northtown, Galesburg, and Eola, Illinois. Some carload traffic was transferred to the massive Clearing Yard just a few miles away.

Finding the yard is not difficult. Cicero lies 7 miles due west of downtown Chicago, on the north side of Ogden Boulevard. Road access is good, and two road overpasses formerly afforded good views of activity in the complex. Traveling from Chicago, these were right turns at Laramie Street or Austin Boulevard. The first gave good views over the neck of the old hump yard. The second was a good spot to observe departures from the yard.

By 2002, however, the transformation to a TOFC and COFC facility rendered all signs of the old hump yard invisible. The view from Laramie is unrecognizable from the images taken in 1995, and the Austin Boulevard Bridge has been demolished.

This is the view looking east from the Cicero hump tower. In May 1995, the 17 arrival tracks were still intact and had a good variety of carload traffic, generally collected in local industry jobs and assembled at Cicero for the long haul to places like Galesburg and Minneapolis. To the left and right of the reception yard, the new trailers-on-flatcars (TOFC) and containers-on-flatcars (COFC) facilities can be seen. Double-stack and autorack traffic also is seen encroaching on the reception yard—a sign of things to come at Cicero.

# Corwith Yard—Chicago, Illinois

With the merger of Burlington Northern and Santa Fe in 1994-95, BN gained two large, mechanized classification yards, Argentine and Barstow, and several other flat yards. One of these, the Corwith facility in Chicago, had been a traditional hump classification yard until the late 1970s, dedicated to carload traffic with 34 classification tracks. However, Santa Fe had transformed most of the land occupied by Corwith into Chicago's largest intermodal yard. It remains frenetically busy, with up to 40 intermodal departures per 24 hours.

Road access to Corwith is poor, providing little opportunity to view the yard from a public place. Official yard access is from 38th Street. Turn left off Western and pass under the railroad at the north end of the yard. The road curves to the left, where the main yard office is located.

Four Santa Fe warbonnets reverse into the yard at Corwith in May 1995. This view was taken from the north end of the yard. The locomotives will take a TOFC train west, one of more than 20 daily departures from Corwith, which was BNSF's main intermodal depot in 1995. Since then, the 250-acre site at Cicero has been transformed into a second and somewhat larger BNSF intermodal yard for the Chicago area.

The original Galesburg Yard, a CB&Q facility built in the 1940s, contained two hump yards. BN began modernizing the yard in 1982 and completed the new, automated Galesburg hump yard in October 1984. It covered 943 acres and cost $80 million.

Five arrival and departure roads were placed alongside the hump bowl, which had 32 classification tracks. Hump shunting was effected by drawing back arrivals from their road to a single shunting lead. Although this is by no means the most efficient layout for a yard, up to 1,600 cars were classified every 24 hours. Forty manifest trains passed through the yard every day, and BNSF management argued that the theoretical hump capacity was 2,500 cars per day. This was partly because, at 4,000 feet, the classification tracks were unusually long.

With the merger of BN and Santa Fe, Galesburg assumed increased importance as the key yard at the eastern end of the empire. In 1995, a new retarder system was installed, and another eight classification tracks were added. An additional eight classification tracks followed in 1996, bringing the bowl up to 48 roads. Two more arrival and departure roads, each 7,500 feet long, also were added.

Even with this expansion, in order to cope with increased throughput and a larger number of destinations for freight cars, further expansion was to come. In 1997, a $24.5-million scheme aimed to add 14 more classification tracks and two more arrival and departure roads, bringing the yard to 62 tracks and into the top three yards on the BNSF, along with Northtown and Argentine.

The yard lies about 3 miles southwest of the town center and is easy to view. To reach the long overpass that crosses the exit from the classification bowl, exit U.S. Highway 34 at Main Street. Head south into Galesburg, and after a mile or so, before crossing the railroad, turn right onto Henderson. Travel for nearly 3 miles and you will reach a T-junction, where a left turn leads you across the yard. Traffic is light on the overpass, and there is room for parking. It is important to note that through traffic, including large numbers of intermodal trains, bypasses the yard.

By May 1995, BNSF's plan to expand Galesburg into the major eastern classification yard for the new super railroad was well underway. Cars roll over the hump into the 32 classification tracks, while the bulldozers have cleared and prepared land for another 16 classification tracks. Compare this view with the next picture—taken in 2002, when all the tracks are in use.

ABOVE: Cars roll down the hump at Galesburg in 1995. At the time, the yard classified 1,600 cars per day but had the capacity to handle 2,500.

LEFT: In 2002, BNSF introduced trainpacks for their yard crews. Here, an engineer is seen with his train controller suspended around his neck as he drives his locomotive from the front walkway. These new trainpacks have been used in Europe for more than a decade and greatly increase productivity in and around yards.

BELOW: BNSF No. 6104 draws autoracks out of the classification bowl at Galesburg. On the right are the 16 new tracks added in 1995. Several BNSF locomotives are employed on pullout duty on this chilly morning.

For more than 20 years, Northtown has held the crown as the largest yard on the BN system. The merger with Atchison, Topeka & Santa Fe (ATSF) and the incorporation of a rebuilt Argentine Yard into the network mean that these two yards vie for superiority, but Argentine is undoubtedly busier than its northern cousin. Northtown was built on the site of the old Northern Pacific (NP) Yard in Minneapolis and cost $43 million. Construction stretched from 1971 to 1976 and included not only the hump classification yard but also a large engine house and a car-repair facility.

At the time, the 12 reception sidings held 1,472 cars. Sixty-three classification tracks and nine departure roads held 1,484 cars. In addition, 27 sidings accommodated local traffic, with a combined capacity of 1,026 cars. This massive new facility so simplified switching operations in the Twin Cities that it had paid for itself by 1978.

The Northtown terminal saw 100 trains every day in 1998. Not all were manifest services, however, and many unit trains or intermodal services whistled past the yard. In 1998, there were daily manifests to Grand Forks, Chicago, Tulsa, Memphis, Galesburg, Minot, and Winnipeg, not to mention numerous local switching and transfer workings.

All was not well at the big yard in 1999, however. Throughput of cars had fallen from the target of 2,000 per day to just 600. Labor unrest and BNSF's determination to cut its dependence on classification yards found many manifests being routed away from the yard. By pre-blocking cars from the Dakotas, the need for reclassification at Northtown has been abolished. This means that only three long-distance manifests originated at Northtown in mid-2000. Two fans of eight classification tracks were mothballed, reducing the number of tracks in the bowl from 64 to 48. The long-term future of the yard seems in doubt.

Yard activity is easily observed from two very good overpasses. Forty-fourth Avenue NE runs over the yard just north of the hump itself and close to the Northtown Engine House. To the south, the St. Anthony Parkway crosses the departure end of the yard, where yard pullouts may be observed. The view of the body of the yard is obscured by the Soo Railroad, which crosses the south end of Northtown about 200 yards north of the St. Anthony Parkway.

The view of Northtown, looking north from St. Anthony Parkway, shows BNSF No. 6102 on pullout duty as a long manifest departs south.

Six of the eight secondary retarders are seen in this view of the classification bowl at Northtown in Minneapolis. Each is equipped with green-painted shielding to protect the retarders from Minnesota snowfalls. The triple engine lash-up was on hump pilot duty on this day in July 1989. The locomotives have completed the sorting of an inbound manifest. Now they must travel over the hump themselves, to propel cars well into the classification tracks that have run too slowly and stopped short of their allotted positions.

This view was taken from the CP overpass to the south of Northtown. Yard slug No. 6117 waits to pull cars out of the bowl. The hump tower is visible in the background. The busy CP line from which this was taken was closed due to bridge work.

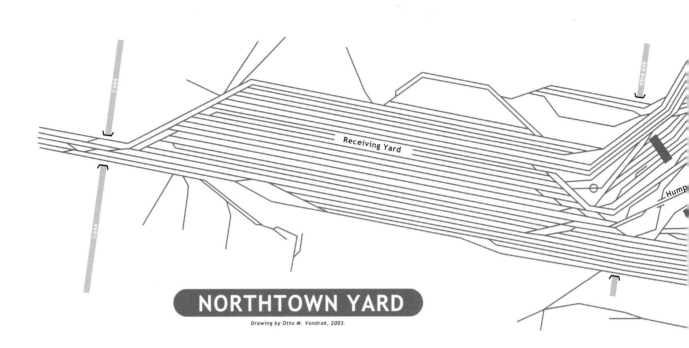

# NORTHTOWN YARD

*Drawing by Otto M. Vondrak, 2003.*

Standing on 44th Avenue gives one a good overall view, both north and south, of Northtown. Looking south in October 2002, a BNSF manifest leaves the yard. In the background is the Minneapolis skyline, while to the left is the classification bowl and on the extreme left is the hump crest.

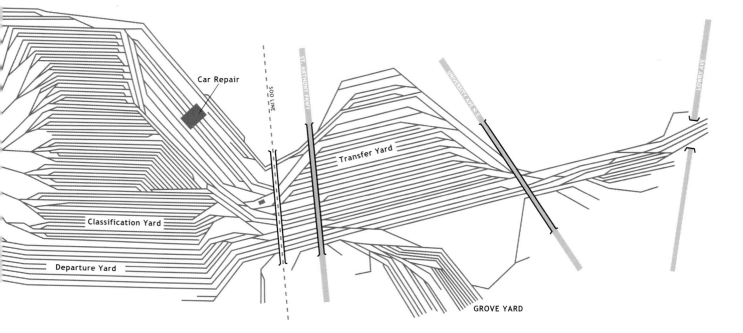

Car Repair

Classification Yard

Departure Yard

SOO LINE

ST. ANTHONY AVE

Transfer Yard

UNIVERSITY AVE

LOWRY AVE

GROVE YARD

# Minot Gavin Yard—Minot, North Dakota

This Great Northern Yard was built in the early 1950s, primarily to classify the numerous grain cars from North and South Dakota branchlines. Nine arrival and departure tracks led to 40 classification roads. The yard continues in use today, although less important than it was in Great Northern days. The hump closed in the 1980s, and the remnants of the classification bowl are mainly used to store block trains of grain cars. Sixteen tracks remain, eight of them long enough to hold full trains and eight somewhat shorter, which are used to classify cars. The whole yard lies in open country, 5 miles due east of Minot, and is easy to see from the surrounding countryside.

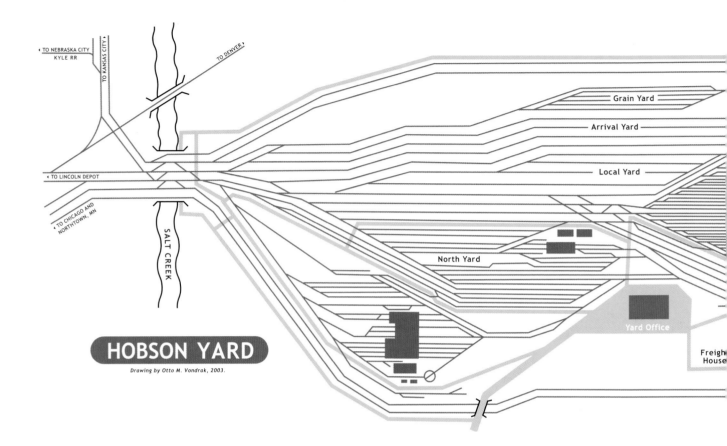

TO NEBRASKA CITY
KYLE RR

TO KANSAS CITY

TO DENVER

TO LINCOLN DEPOT

TO CHICAGO AND
NORTHTOWN, MN

SALT CREEK

Grain Yard

Arrival Yard

Local Yard

North Yard

Yard Office

Freight
House

## HOBSON YARD

*Drawing by Otto M. Vondrak, 2003.*

This yard dates back to 1906. The modern hump yard is the result of a $1.3-million investment by the CB&Q in 1944. A rise in traffic came to Lincoln in the 1970s as a result of Powder River coal, but the number of cars that needed classifying fell. At its busiest in the 1950s, 5,000 carloads each day passed through Hobson, the majority of which needed remarshaling. Today, up to 70 trains every day pass through Lincoln, but 50 of these are unit coal trains (25 loaded and 25 empties). The number of cars needing classification has fallen to just 900.

The crunch for Lincoln and its hump yard came in 1994, when the retarder equipment needed refurbishing. This scale of investment was hard to justify when the majority of traffic at Hobson was unit trains and intermodal. Most railroad companies, when faced with this situation over the last 25 years, have simply abolished the hump in a yard and reverted to flat-switching.

However, this was not the case at Hobson Yard. Mike Weisman, the yard superintendent at the time, had HBR

Associates advise on the best course of action. Their man for the job, Andy Andersen, had worked for Union Pacific (UP) at the time Livonia Yard in Louisiana was designed and built.

Livonia was the first U.S. yard to employ Dowty retarders (described in the Livonia Yard entry in Chapter 2). These tiny, rail-side cylinders require less maintenance than traditional rail-brake retarders and allow more rapid classification of cars. The hump at Lincoln was therefore converted to a Dowty retarder hump and now classifies 900 cars per day into 32 tracks. The yard also has four arrival and four departure tracks, each capable of holding 120 to 135 cars. Also, wrapped around the outside of the yard are three run-through tracks on the north side and four on the south. These are designed to ease the passage of coal traffic around the yard and allow locomotives to refuel and change crews without snarling the operation of the manifest yard. They have been successful in relieving congestion at Lincoln, and four more are planned in the near future.

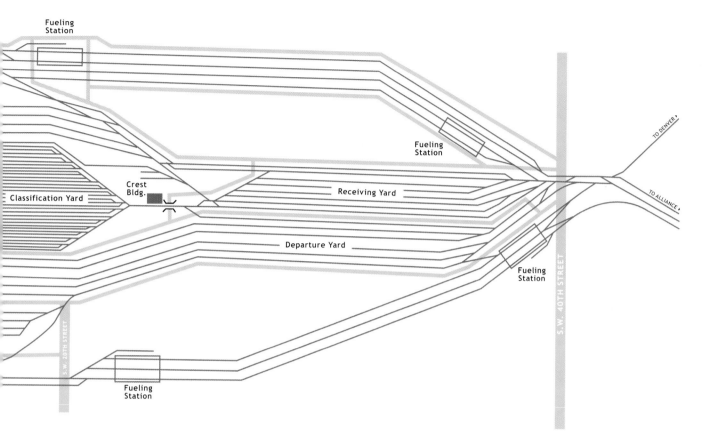

Fueling
Station

Crest
Bldg.

Classification Yard

Receiving Yard

Fueling
Station

TO DENVER

TO ALLIANCE

S.W. 40TH STREET

Departure Yard

Fueling
Station

S.W. 20TH STREET

Fueling
Station

Even though coal traffic dominates the railroad at Hobson Yard, there are still 17 to 20 daily manifest jobs. Six locals run out and back to locations less than 100 miles from Lincoln, and seven daily long-distance freights go to Minneapolis, Galesburg, Kansas City, Denver, Pasco, Tulsa, and Casper, Wyoming. Each has a balancing inbound working every 24 hours. On top of this are run-through TOFC and COFC trains, making Lincoln one of the best places to watch BNSF in action.

Access to the yard is good, with crossings at both the west and east ends of the facility and an excellent (if somewhat busy) road overpass in the middle of the yard. Sunvalley Street runs along the northern border of the yard, and at the east end, First Street crosses the exit from the yard. There is plenty of public parking and open ground to view activity here and at the west end of the facility, where 40th Street crosses the yard exit. The Homestead Expressway or U.S. Highway 77 crosses right over the hump area and is the best spot to observe the yard.

In October 2002, two tank cars roll over the Dowty retarders at Hobson Yard and into their classification tracks.

The hump engines trim some tracks in the bowl at Hobson Yard. The Nebraska state capitol building in Lincoln is on the horizon, while nearer to the camera, piles of grain that have spilled out of boxcars lie along the tracks.

North and south of Hobson are run-through tracks for the large number of unit coal trains passing through the yard. Here, a train approaches the refueling racks on the north side of the complex in October 2002.

BN had their major yard at Lindenwood in St. Louis, but in 1988, a significant investment in the site saw this facility used mainly for intermodal traffic. Most BN carload traffic passing through the St. Louis area is classified at Madison Yard, which is owned by the Terminal Railroad Association of St. Louis (TRRA). There is an excellent overview of the east end of Lindenwood Yard from Arsenal Street.

Looking west from Arsenal Street, an empty unit coal train passes through Lindenwood Yard in April 2001. Immediately to the right and left of the train are the flat shunted tracks used by manifest traffic. On the far right, the intermodal facility can just be seen—it is located on land previously occupied by a hump yard.

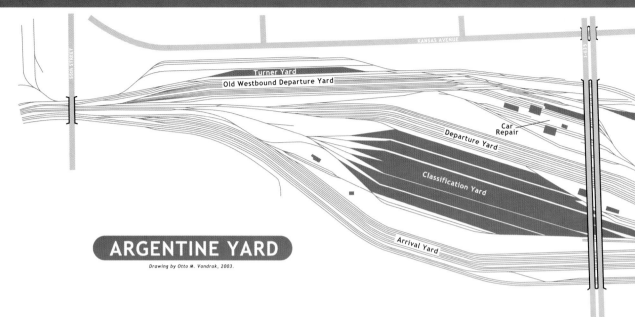

**ARGENTINE YARD**

*Drawing by Otto M. Vondrak, 2003.*

Argentine Yard was the focal point of the entire Santa Fe system. Since the merger of BN and Santa Fe, it has been totally rebuilt and remains one of the top three yards on BNSF.

Freight yards were built on the outskirts of Kansas City at Argentine as long ago as 1906, but the massive, dual-hump yard, which served the Santa Fe, dates from the 1950s. The terminal area sees 5,000 cars pass through every day. Even back in 1996, toward the end for the dual hump, the two humps classified more than 2,000 cars every day. The rest of the cars passing through Argentine were mainly in the form of "hotshot" intermodal traffic, which always paused for a mandatory 1,000-mile inspection and refueling.

The eastbound classification system at Argentine closed in December 1995. It had 23 reception roads, which lay parallel to the classification bowl. Classification worked on the "drawback" principle, as at Galesburg. The bowl had 48 tracks, leading to 14 departure roads. During its final year, the bowl classified 800 cars each day.

The westbound system, in contrast, was laid out in a more traditional manner; 16 reception tracks led to the hump, from where 53 classification tracks radiated. Cars were then drawn forward to one of 14 departure roads.

In 1995, this yard handled 1,200 to 1,400 cars daily. The old Argentine was enormous, with 226 miles of track

This view on the eastern edge of Argentine illustrates the move away from carload traffic. Warbonnet No. 119 heads five high-powered diesels at the head of a LANY (Los Angeles-to-New York) TOFC train that has paused in the yard for refueling and a 1,000-mile inspection. Two eastbound inspection and fueling roads are in almost constant use. Warbonnet No. 618 heads another TOFC, the RICH (Richmond-to-Chicago), on its way east. In the background, various low-powered Santa Fe locomotives are on pullout duty at the east end of the eastbound classification yard.

**Transfer Yard**

**Diesel Shops**

and room for the amazing number of 12,026 cars. BNSF has totally rebuilt the yard to speed throughput of carloads and also to increase the facilities for passing block loads and intermodals.

In July 1997, BNSF opened a new hump, which could handle four cars per minute or a theoretical 5,760 each day. Ten reception roads, up to 8,466 feet long, lie alongside the hump. The hump itself leads to 60 classification tracks, which are unusually long, the longest approaching 8,000 feet. There are 10 departure tracks, again approaching 8,000 feet long. The yard currently classifies 2,400 cars per day and is the first on BNSF to use Dowty retarders.

Argentine is one of the more accessible yards in the United States, with several conveniently placed overpasses. The best of these is reached by exiting I-635 northbound at Metropolitan, heading east, and then immediately turning left onto 44th Street. This crosses the exit from the classification bowl via a 400-yard-long viaduct, which is a quiet

place to watch the trains go by. There are views of the yard from I-635 but no opportunity to stop and watch the trains. In addition, there are bridges over the west end of the complex on 55th Street and over the east end on 18th Street. The east end of the yard also accommodates a large engine house, which can be seen from 18th Street.

Just months before Argentine's closure in December 1995, cars roll down the hump in the eastbound classification yard. The 48 classification tracks were the first to close in the stepwise process that led to the complete rebuild at Argentine. This view was taken from the hump tower in October 1995.

Argentine's larger and more modern east-west hump featured pushbutton classification. The yard control panel is shown here in October 1995.

The yardmaster sits astride his mixture of equipment. Elderly switching and retarder controls are mixed with more modern computers used for train identification and car cutting. In the background, a makeshift corrugated shed is seen on the hump crest, to protect the car cutters from inclement weather.

The westbound classification yard in the old Argentine was larger than the eastbound, with 53 tracks. The classification bowl is seen here from the hump tower in October 1995. This yard was ripped up in 1996 and 1997 to make way for the all-new, 60-track bowl that classified in the eastbound direction.

Most large classification yards include an engine house and a car shop. The carload shop at Argentine is being shunted by BNSF No. 1409 in this view taken from the 44th Street overpass. In the background is Interstate 635, which affords excellent views over the yard but, unfortunately, no place to stop.

The new Argentine is seen here in April 2001. In the distance, the new hump with its corrugated shed can be seen. This leads to 60 classification tracks. Nearer the camera are two pairs of BNSF yard power, used to pull out strings of cars from classification tracks and place them into the departure roads. One full-length departure may accommodate three or four strings of cars from the classification bowl.

# Murray Yard—Kansas City, Missouri

Before the merger with Santa Fe, the main BN yard in Kansas City was to the north of the town and was called Murray Yard. A four-year project in the early 1970s, costing $10 million, led to a 3-mile-long, flat-switched yard being converted into a state-of-the-art hump yard.

Eighteen reception roads with a capacity of 1,632 cars lead over a single hump to a 41-track classification bowl (originally 42 tracks, now reduced to 41). Four departure tracks hold a total of 652 cars. The yard dispatches 20 freights every day and, during a visit in 1995, it was handling 1,500 cars a day over the hump. The theoretical capacity when the yard opened in 1972 was 4,000 cars per day, but this has never been reached.

Although the yard was busy in 1995 and 1996 because of the rebuilding at Argentine, it has now been relegated to an industry transfer yard, and there is talk of complete closure. More likely it will continue as a staging yard for coal traffic from the Powder River Basin on its way south. As one heads north from Kansas City on Broadway, the yard lies on the right, but there are no easy locations for photography.

Cars roll over the hump at Murray Yard in October 1995. This view was taken from the hump tower. Since then, the hump has been bulldozed away and the tracks lengthened to accommodate unit coal traffic. There is no clue as to where the hump used to stand.

Cars roll into the bowl at Murray Yard. The hump tower was fitted with a mirror to allow the yardmaster to view the retarder area as well as the hump crest at the same time. The mirror reflects the author in this view.

# Springfield Yard—Springfield, Missouri

The Frisco Railroad built Springfield Yard—a flat-switched yard with 40 tracks—in the 1950s. While the yard was the busiest on the Frisco, with 43 freight trains passing through each day, it was by no means the largest. The 4,508-mile Frisco system had two large hump yards at Memphis and Tulsa, but Springfield was the hub of the railroad. In the center are 31 classification roads, with the capacity to accommodate 1,900 cars. On either side of this central bowl are four tracks, each holding 150 cars, doubling as both reception and departure roads.

# Memphis Yard—Memphis, Tennessee

The Frisco built Memphis Yard in 1957; 10 arrival and departure tracks were provided along a 60-track bowl. The hump operates on a pullback technique, with two pullback roads leading to the hump. The relentless increase in intermodal traffic led BN to convert tracks 1 through 10 in the classification bowl into a TOFC ramp; the yard operates its carload classification using roads 11 through 60 today. During a visit in 1997, the hump was classifying 1,400 cars each day, while a total of 3,000 cars passed through the Memphis terminal each day.

It is not easy to observe Memphis Yard from a public place. The roads that cross the yard entrance and exits do so as underpasses. The yard lies 8 miles southeast of downtown Memphis and is best found by heading south on Lamar Avenue (U.S. Highway 78) and taking the Raines Road exit to the north. After passing under the railroad, turn right along Hungerford Road. This parallels the yard, giving some views into the facility.

The Memphis Yard bowl is seen from the hump tower. The yard has 50 classification tracks, divided into five groups of 10. The encroachment of TOFC traffic onto land previously used by manifest trains can be seen in the background, where 10 classification tracks have been replaced by an intermodal facility. This has left the classification bowl asymmetrical.

# Cherokee Yard—Tulsa, Oklahoma

Cherokee Yard is the second largest on the old Frisco, after Memphis. The yard was opened in 1960 and has four arrival tracks, a 41-track classification bowl, and six departure roads. The yard is busy and during a visit on May 21, 1998, more than 1,701 cars had been over the hump in the previous 24 hours, with 1,675 cars sent out on a total of 17 departures.

Tulsa Yard is very accessible. It lies to the left of I-244 as one heads north into Tulsa. Take the 21st/23rd Street exit and head west. An excellent overpass permits observation of the yard's operation.

Looking south at Tulsa's Cherokee Yard from the 21st Street overpass just after dawn. Two BNSF yard slugs draw cars out of the classification bowl, while two other yard jobs are in the hands of yellow ex–Santa Fe power.

The Cherokee bowl is seen to good effect from the hump tower. The hump engines are down in the bowl, trimming cars that have stopped short of their classification track.

P asco was chosen as the site for the first NP hump yard and opened in 1955. The site had been home to an NP yard since 1884. The 1955 hump yard was extensively modified between 1969 and 1971. The receiving yard was enlarged from three to five tracks, while the hump was fitted with a new computer. The 47-track classification bowl remained the same, as did the six departure roads.

The early 1970s were a period of confusion for the BN in the Pacific Northwest. In 1972, work began on a new classification yard at Hauser, near Spokane. This was to have been a yard with a 76-track bowl, the biggest on the BN, but it was never completed. Pasco remains the major carload yard in the Pacific Northwest.

Throughout the 1990s, Pasco has steadily classified approximately 50,000 cars each month and acted as the main gateway to Portland, Tacoma, and Seattle. A visit in 1996 revealed that 1,700 cars had been over the hump on the previous day, and the yard had sent out 14 long-distance manifests as well as four locals. The reopening of Stampede Pass further strengthens Pasco's key role in classifying carload traffic, and improvements continue at the yard.

Like many yards in rural areas, the facility at Pasco is easily seen from neighboring roads. The yard lies northwest of the town's center.

The original 1955 switching equipment is still used at Pasco—it looks a little incongruous against the backdrop of modern, high-capacity freight cars.

It's 6:00 A.M. and time for a shift change on the hump engines resting beneath the hump at Pasco. A string of cars approaches the hump above the two pairs of locomotives that form the two other hump jobs of the morning.

BN locomotives Nos. 6126 and 6194 rest between turns at the west end of Pasco Yard. This view shows just how short the classification tracks are at Pasco, with many holding as few as 30 cars. It also emphasizes the use of older locomotives around yards. Many of the railroad's oldest machines are to be found in switching yards.

The classification bowl at Pasco, seen from the yard tower in 1996.

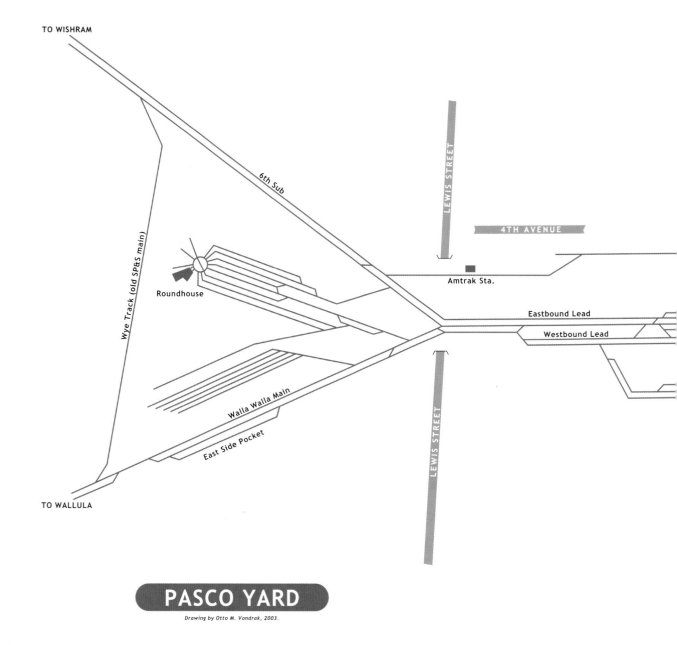

TO WISHRAM

6th Sub

Wye Track (old SP&S main)

Roundhouse

LEWIS STREET

4TH AVENUE

Amtrak Sta.

Eastbound Lead

Westbound Lead

Walla Walla Main

East Side Pocket

LEWIS STREET

TO WALLULA

## PASCO YARD

*Drawing by Otto M. Vondrak, 2003.*

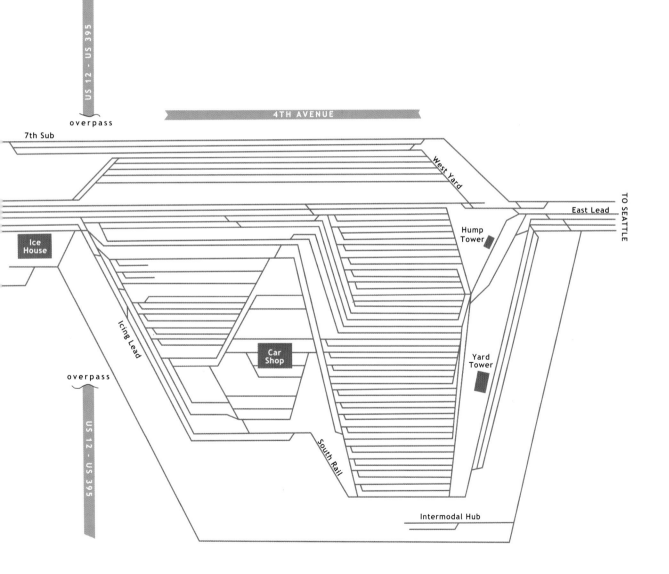

US 12 - US 395

overpass

7th Sub

4TH AVENUE

West Yard

TO SEATTLE

East Lead

Hump Tower

Ice House

Icing Lead

Car Shop

Yard Tower

overpass

US 12 - US 395

South Rail

Intermodal Hub

Most carload traffic for the West Coast is classified and pre-blocked in Pasco, but Seattle has a small classification yard at Interbay, also known as Balmer. The yard is perhaps the smallest hump yard on BNSF, with just 16 tracks in the bowl, and short tracks at that. A single mechanical retarder controlled the descent of cars from the tiny hump but was removed in 1994. With the closure of other car-classifying facilities, such as the yard at Auburn, Interbay is surprisingly busy. The yard and adjacent engine house are easy to observe from Dravus Street, which spans the middle of the yard, between 15th and 20th Streets.

RIGHT: An empty unit grain train passes Interbay Yard. During the harvest season, the yard is often crammed full of grain cars because both Seattle and Tacoma are important export points for North American grain.

The tiny, 16-track bowl at Interbay (Balmer) Yard is seen here in 1996. Several tracks are out of use pending repairs. The yard's erstwhile retarder is lying in bits adjacent to the photographer, out of sight in this view.

The major BNSF yard in California is in the Mojave Desert, at Barstow (pop 24,000). Santa Fe built the yard in 1971, and it remains the key classification point for all carload traffic to the Los Angeles Basin and also to northern California, via Tehachapi.

At the time it opened, Santa Fe boasted mechanized hump yards at Corwith (Chicago), Argentine (Kansas City), and Pueblo (Colorado). The new yard cost $50 million and was laid out in a conventional fashion, with 10 receiving tracks, a 48-track bowl, and 10 departure tracks.

The receiving tracks were well spaced, with 22 feet between them for the cars' cutters to scoot along the train. Total capacity of the receiving yard is 1,420 cars. The bowl can hold just over 2,000 cars, while the departure yard has a capacity of 1,370.

During a visit in 1992, the hump classified 1,200 cars in a 24-hour period, but a noticeable number of intermodal cars were switched over the hump. On top of that was an endless flow of Santa Fe intermodal trains passing the yard on the way to the Los Angeles Basin. Besides this, more than 20 UP freights from nearby Yermo Yard passed by each day. The yard remains busy with carload traffic since the BNSF merger, but this work is overshadowed by the ceaseless flow of through traffic at Barstow.

By far the best place to get a sense of the size and scale of the yard is from Barstow Hill. This hill lies at the east end of the yard and rises adjacent to North Street, the main road through Barstow. Otherwise, eastbound departures from the yard can be seen well from First Avenue in Barstow. Traveling out from Barstow to the east along I-40, the BNSF and UP mainlines lie to the north of the roadway. Numerous grade crossings intersect the old single-track road that runs parallel to the highway.

In the background on the right is Barstow Hill. This view was taken from the hump tower at Barstow and shows a string of cars rolling down the hump. To the right, a couple of TOFC cars have been placed to one side. They are not cleared for hump shunting and will be picked up by the hump engine once all the manifest traffic has been classified. They will then be placed manually into the classification bowl, to avoid any damage to or movement of the road vehicles they convey.

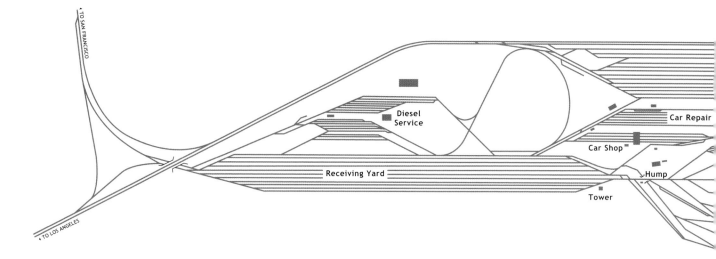

Looking west from Barstow Hill, the Santa Fe yard stretches out to infinity. The geometry of the classification bowl can be appreciated from this elevated location.

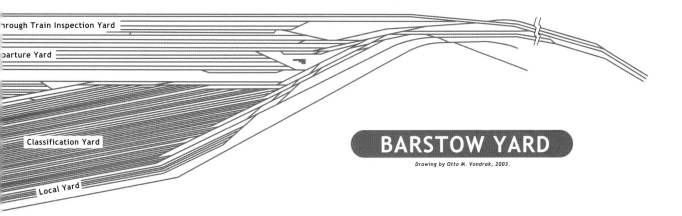

Through Train Inspection Yard

Departure Yard

Classification Yard

Local Yard

## BARSTOW YARD

*Drawing by Otto M. Vondrak, 2003.*

Intermodal makes up the majority of BNSF traffic passing through Barstow. Here, a relatively short train bound for the Los Angeles Basin accelerates west from the yard in 1992, when the Santa Fe Railroad still owned the facility.

I may say that the sprawling, flat-switched yard in Birmingham, Alabama, deserves a mention. On the other hand, the 38th Street Yard in Denver received a $5.5-million refurbishment in 1975, and the flat yard there boasts nearly 50 tracks. Finally, there are the yards at Alliance in Nebraska. This collection of yards broke the 100 barrier for daily train throughput back in 1981 and is one of BN's busiest locations, thanks to Powder River coal.

The Denver skyline forms the backdrop to this 1995 view of the 38th Street Yard. An empty unit coal train passes the yard on its way back to the Powder River Basin.

The name of the game in Alliance, Nebraska, is coal. This view of the main yard shows two loaded coal trains in the loops and an empty coal train passing as an intermodal fills the final loop. There is some trackage for carload traffic, but it is small compared to the miles of track built to handle Powder River coal.

The original Union Pacific (UP) was a much smaller railroad than the behemoth it is today. Mergers and acquisitions have made UP the biggest railroad in the United States. Originally, UP had a solitary hump yard at North Platte, in 1948. The yard at Pocatello (Idaho) was built on original UP territory, as was the relative newcomer at Hinkle (Oregon). The rest of the major yards listed under the modern-day UP have their parenthood in other railroads.

The Missouri Pacific (MoPac) has contributed the hump yards in Kansas City, Fort Worth, and North Little Rock, while the Chicago & North Western brought the massive Proviso Yard to the UP stable. Takeover of the Alton and Southern brought St. Louis Gateway Yard under sole UP ownership, while merger with SP added even more yards.

The merger with SP was perhaps the biggest incremental change in the size of the UP and also had the biggest impact on the yards operated by the railroad. Roseville was inherited from SP in a dangerous state and was totally re-built, while West Colton was in much better shape and works unchanged under UP ownership. Yards at Strang, Englewood, and Pine Bluff also are SP-built. This leaves just one major yard unaccounted for, at Livonia, Louisiana, where UP built a new, state-of-the-art yard for petrochemical traffic around Baton Rouge.

A local dock job passes the entrance to Strang Yard with a short train of double-stack containers.

than 2 million. The transport needs of the rapidly growing city were catered largely by the railroads. The UP built a new yard in Los Angeles, called East Yard, on a 230-acre site. A 1,000-car receiving yard was supplemented by a 700-car eastbound classification yard and an 880-car westbound classification yard.

During the next 30 years, the yard was gradually expanded, with the addition of a yard to handle local trip freights, carriage sidings, and extensions to the locomotive depot. Perhaps the most important event during this 30-year phase, however, was the arrival of the first-ever piggyback service in 1953. During the 1960s, a piggyback ramp was added at East Yard, permitting more efficient unloading of trailers.

In 1970, UP invested another $2.8 million in East Yard when the company converted the B Yard, which had previously handled locals, into a 16-track automated hump yard. The next decade saw a dramatic increase in the volume of TOFC and COFC traffic passing through

gridlock in Los Angeles. East Yard was now hemmed in by residential development, so UP selected a "greenfield" site for its new southern California yard, Yermo. In fact, the term "fresh desert" might better describe Yermo, which is situated a few miles from Barstow in the Mojave Desert (see below).

In 1977, the C Yard, which had been used for eastbound traffic, was replaced by parking space for trailers. Asphalt advanced again when, in 1987, the size of the intermodal yard was doubled, making it the largest on the UP system. Seven tracks accommodate TOFC and double-stack traffic. The surrounding area, once occupied by steel rails, is now asphalt, with a capacity to park more than 2,000 trailers. In 1990, the hump yard, opened just 20 years earlier, was decommissioned because most classification of carload traffic was effectively handled at Yermo. The engine house at East Yard remains the only maintenance facility for locomotives because the closest shops are in Salt Lake City, 784 miles away.

# Taylor Yard—Glendale, California

Taylor Yard, formerly the major SP classification facility in Los Angeles, is now no more than a wide expanse of ballast, with the new commuter train depot parked on its southern extremity. It was once one of the major SP yards boasting 36 classification tracks. According to employees with whom I spoke during a visit in 1992, use of the yard had been waning until SP could complete a new facility at West Colton. Closure started in 1985, and by 1992, nothing was left of the 24-track reception yard, 36 classification tracks, and 12 departure roads. Only the SP locomotive shops remained, and these closed in 1998, replaced by a large facility adjacent to West Colton Yard. This brought an end to SP's facilities in downtown Los Angeles.

This view shows the vast SP engine house at Taylor Yard in Glendale, California. Behind the SD45 with wearing the ill-fated SPSF livery lies the wasteland that resulted from the yard's closure in 1992.

Between 1980 and 1981, UP constructed a new yard at Yermo to classify carload traffic bound for the Los Angeles Basin. The 24-track yard cost $9 million and had room for 1,500 cars. By 1993, the yard was responsible for switching 35,000 cars per month. This was almost as many as the nearby Barstow Yard, owned by the ATSF, but Barstow was blessed with much more extensive facilities and hump operation. UP also chose to provide fueling and inspection roads for TOFC, COFC, and unit trains.

Four tracks pass a modern fueling pad, which can accommodate six locomotives on each of its four bays and fuel up to 16 locomotives simultaneously. Yermo was responsible for all carload classification in southern California between 1981 and 1996, as it was the only major classification yard on the UP between Salt Lake City and Los Angeles. After a merger with SP, however, Yermo became a holding point for TOFC and COFC cars, while the former SP yard at West Colton became the carload yard for southern California.

A Los Angeles-bound manifest joins the BNSF mainline at Dagget, 3 miles west of Yermo. For the trip from Yermo down to San Bernardino, Union Pacific traffic parallels the BNSF through Barstow Yard and down the Cajon Pass, making this route one of the busiest in the United States.

West Colton was built by the Southern Pacific (SP) in 1972 as its major Los Angeles Basin yard. Once it opened, the writing was on the wall for the older SP yard at Taylor in Glendale.

West Colton itself is 6 miles long and was built with more than 100 miles of track, laid out conventionally with nine reception roads at the west end, with a capacity to hold 1,800 cars. These lead over a single-track hump to 48 classification tracks, which vary in length from 2,400 to 3,300 feet. The fully automated hump has a 6 percent slope and can handle up to eight cars a minute. However, during March 1993, the throughput was a steady 1,600 cars per day.

Adjacent to the classification tracks are the car repair and locomotive servicing facilities, which have recently been expanded to replace the shops at Taylor Yard. Departure is from one of 14 sidings, which can hold a total of 2,000 cars. Interestingly, all departures leave from the east end of the yard, even those going west. Westbound traffic traverses a "balloon track" to make the 180-degree change of direction to head back into the Los Angeles Basin.

In 1993, 15 long-distance manifests were built each day in the yard. With merger to UP, traffic increased. UP is currently expanding the yard with the construction of 16 more classification tracks. Just as in northern California, where Roseville has been rebuilt as the main UP/SP facility, West Colton is the major carload yard for the duo in southern California. Carload work previously carried out at East Yard and Yermo will now be concentrated at West Colton, leaving the other yards to focus on servicing container and unit trains.

The yard is blessed with several excellent spots from which to observe activity. Traveling along I-10 westbound, take the Riverside Avenue exit in San Bernardino. Turn south along here, and a quiet overpass permits observation of the east end of the yard.

As well as through traffic, engines leaving the refueling point, and all departures, pass this way. Farther west along I-10 is an exit for Cedar Avenue. Again turn south along here for a bridge over the hump area and also the official entrance to the yard, which is left off Cedar Avenue.

West Colton Yard was built in 1972 and now handles all wagonload traffic to and from the Los Angeles Basin. In addition to the overpasses at either end of the yard, a footbridge provides public access halfway along the yard and is the location for this view, taken in 1993. The afternoon transfer from the Santa Fe Yard in San Bernardino is seen winding out of the classification tracks with cars for the Santa Fe. This footbridge is found by traveling west along Valley Boulevard and taking a left turn on to Cactus Avenue. Within 100 yards are a parking lot and the footbridge into the yard.

The Los Angeles Basin smog is at its dingiest on this day in May 2000. The hump pilots at West Colton are seen pulling a rake of cars out of the classification bowl for re-humping. Sometimes, when complex marshaling of cars is needed, one of the classification tracks is allocated for cars that will need re-humping once other tracks in the bowl are cleared.

Back in 1993, well before the merger with UP, the Southern Pacific was distinguished by its long, rambling manifest traffic. Here, 150 cars start the descent down the Cajon Pass on the way to West Colton Yard.

The view from the Riverside Avenue overpass in May 2000 reveals two local manifests awaiting departure from West Colton. A UP double-stack train passes on the through tracks, with containers from Long Beach for the East.

SP No. 5302 draws a rake of cars from the southern half of the classification tracks at West Colton on March 9, 1993. The cars will be placed in one of 14 departure sidings that have a combined capacity of 2,000 cars.

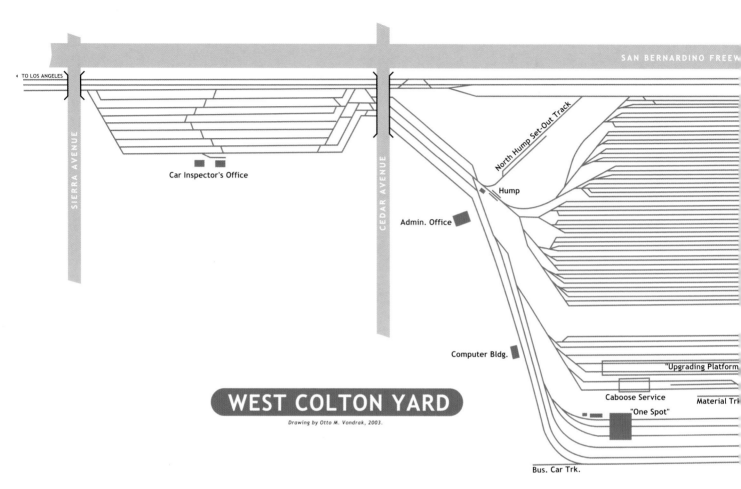

‹ TO LOS ANGELES

SIERRA AVENUE

CEDAR AVENUE

Car Inspector's Office

North Hump Set-Out Track

Hump

Admin. Office

Computer Bldg.

"Upgrading Platform

Caboose Service

Material Trk

"One Spot"

Material Trk

Bus. Car Trk.

# WEST COLTON YARD

*Drawing by Otto M. Vondrak, 2003.*

Taken from the control tower on March 9, 1993, this view of West Colton shows the 48 classification roads. In the background, a lash-up of six locomotives approaches the reception sidings. The mixed freight contains another 182 wagons to be sorted over the hump, which currently operates near its daily capacity of 1,600 cars.

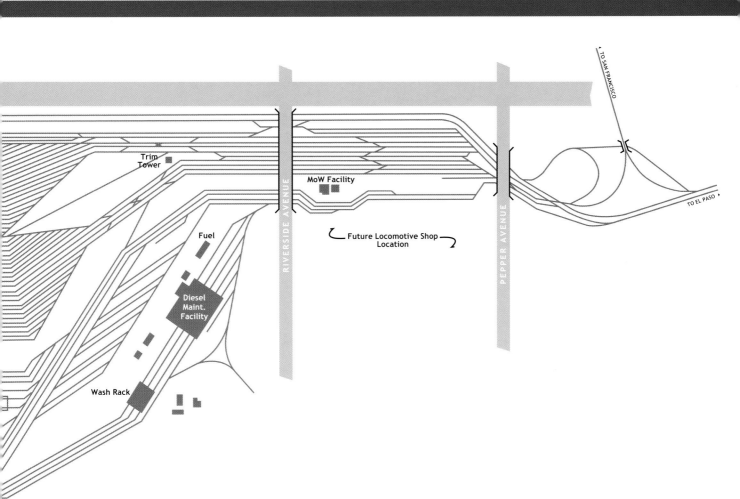

Trim
Tower

MoW Facility

RIVERSIDE AVENUE

Fuel

Future Locomotive Shop
Location

PEPPER AVENUE

TO SAN FRANCISCO

TO EL PASO

Diesel
Maint.
Facility

Wash Rack

# Eugene Yard—Eugene, Oregon

When the yard opened on its present site in 1960, it was the biggest in Oregon. With 32 classification tracks and 10 departure roads, it handled 80 trains every 24 hours. Southern Pacific downgraded the facility such that in the 1980s, the number of classification tracks was reduced to 16. With the 1996 UP/SP merger, the yard's importance decreased further, and in 1999 it was downgraded to a local yard, with the hump and retarders removed. Major classification work previously handled at the yard is now handled at the new Roseville Yard.

The UP hump yard at Hinkle owes its location to two factors. First is the construction, in 1949, of the Mc-Nary Dam on the Columbia River. This caused the UP to have to reroute its tracks, and consideration was given to building a yard in the area. The second factor was Joseph T. Hinkle, the Umatilla County district attorney, whose lobbying efforts influenced the yard's location. The yard was then named after Mr. Hinkle—hence no town called Hinkle is to be found in the atlas.

In 1951, at a cost of $41 million, 41 tracks were laid out as a flat yard. The facility was located to deal with carload traffic to and from the Pacific Northwest. In 1956, a yardmaster's tower was added, and in 1957, extra tracks were laid to cope with growing traffic. It was not until 1976 that the modern hump yard was built. Over a two-year period, $20 million was invested to build a state-of-the-art hump yard, similar in design and outlook to the westbound yard at North Platte.

Today, Hinkle employs 300 people and is being expanded again to facilitate better locomotive refueling and repairs. Most of the current $30-million investment is being used to build a modern engine house to act as UP's main servicing point in the Northwest.

The yard itself classifies all westbound manifests and originates 10 manifest freights per day. A significant number of trains are run-throughs from Portland and Seattle, most of which are COFC or TOFC workings. These stop at Hinkle for crew changes or refueling. The classification yard has 6 arrival tracks and 7 departure tracks, arranged alongside the 40-track bowl. The hump operates on a pullback principle and classifies between 1,200 and 1,500 cars each day.

The yard lies 3 miles south of Hermiston, Oregon. To get there, take the Hermiston exit off I-84 northbound. Within a mile is a country road off to the right, which winds along to the yard area. There are no public overpasses, but activity may be observed from the plentiful open land nearby.

The engine house at Hinkle is the only major UP maintenance facility in the Northwest. The only other major facility in the West lies in northern California, at Roseville.

The UP mainline past Hinkle handles a large volume of unit trains and COFC traffic on its way to and from the Pacific Northwest. In May 1996, a Chicago & North Western Dash 8 and a six-axle UP machine pass the locomotive servicing point with a double-stack bound for Portland.

The classification bowl at Hinkle is viewed here from the hump control room. Its similarity to the westbound classification bowl at Bailey Yard in North Platte gives away its parentage as "modern UP." The bowl has 40 classification tracks which, like many more modern yards, hold up to 80 cars each.

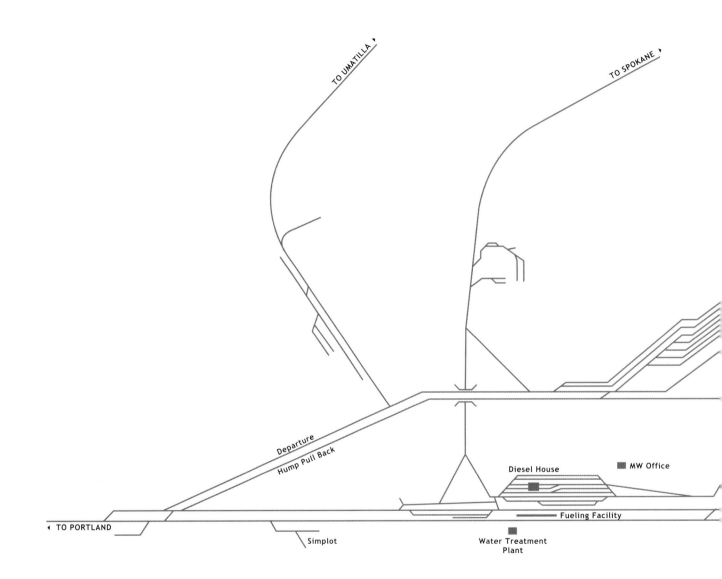

TO UMATILLA ►

TO SPOKANE ►

Departure

Hump Pull Back

Diesel House

■ MW Office

Fueling Facility

◄ TO PORTLAND

Simplot

■ Water Treatment
Plant

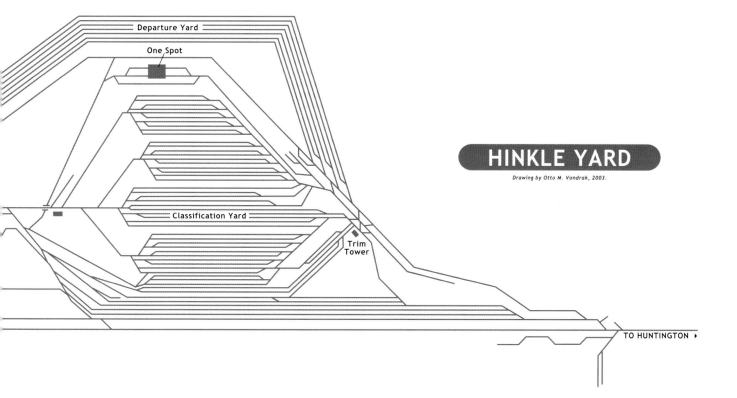

Departure Yard

One Spot

HINKLE YARD

Drawing by Otto M. Vondrak, 2003.

Classification Yard

Trim
Tower

TO HUNTINGTON ▸

# Davis Yard—Roseville, California

In 1952, SP opened the first push-button hump yard in Roseville. Called Jennings Yard, it comprised 21 receiving tracks, 49 classification tracks, and 21 departure roads. Like many yards built during the 1950s, it possessed fairly short classification tracks, most of which could hold no more than 30 cars.

By 1992, only half the classification tracks were in use, and as few as 800 cars a day were sorted over the hump. The 24 roads on the south side of the bowl had been disconnected from the double hump. Three roads from the original south side had been reconnected to one of the northern group retarders, making an uneven split in the yard. Carload freight was in decline, nowhere more obviously than on the SP.

With the merger of SP and UP in 1996, the Roseville Yard was selected as the key yard for Northern California. UP began to completely rebuild it, and it was finished in May 1999 at a cost of $142 million. The transformation at the yard, renamed Davis Yard in 1998, is amazing, with hardly a single piece of track from the old yard left in place.

The new yard employs Dowty retarders rather than the more traditional hydraulic rail brakes found in the majority of hump yards. The 780-acre yard has 8 receiving tracks, 55 classification tracks, and 8 departure tracks. The striking difference from the old yard is the increased length of receiving, departure, and classification roads. The average length of classification tracks is 2,750 feet, and several of the roads in the center of the bowl can handle 80 cars. Receiving

A mixture of SP and leased units occupy the tracks adjacent to the fueling area at Roseville engine house. This view was taken in May 1992.

A general view of the Roseville bowl from the old retarder tower in 1992 shows the unused classification tracks, nearest the camera. It was here that an unexploded bomb was discovered during redevelopment.

The yard's capacity has risen from a maximum of 1,400 cars with the old hump to 2,000 cars per day. In October 1999, the car count for the previous 24 hours had been 1,800. Carload traffic, which was marshaled in Eugene and Stockton, now is concentrated at the Roseville Yard. Eugene and Stockton now handle only local traffic. The hump at Eugene will close as a result of the Roseville expansion.

The yard is easily found by leaving I-80 at the Roseville exit, 10 miles or so past Sacramento, on the way to Reno. The yard dominates the town on the north side and is crossed by several streets, which make excellent observation points. Unfortunately, fine-mesh protective fencing has been erected, which prevents picture taking, but the yard can be seen well from Foothills Boulevard.

and departure yards average 9,000 feet and therefore have been placed on either side of the classification bowl rather than in line with it.

The engine servicing facility remains almost unchanged since SP days and includes 11 sidings for local traffic, 3 for maintenance of way, and 4 for one-spot car repair. There is also room to add 5 extra classification tracks, 4 receiving and departure tracks, and 11 one-spot repair tracks.

The view west from the retarder tower at Roseville shows the old "dual" hump, with two primary retarders. Only the far track was in use at this time.

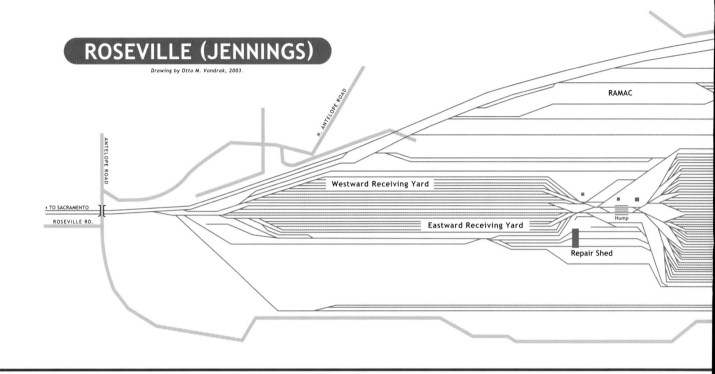

# ROSEVILLE (JENNINGS)

*Drawing by Otto M. Vondrak, 2003.*

ANTELOPE ROAD

N. ANTELOPE ROAD

RAMAC

‹ TO SACRAMENTO

ROSEVILLE RD.

Westward Receiving Yard

Eastward Receiving Yard

Hump

Repair Shed

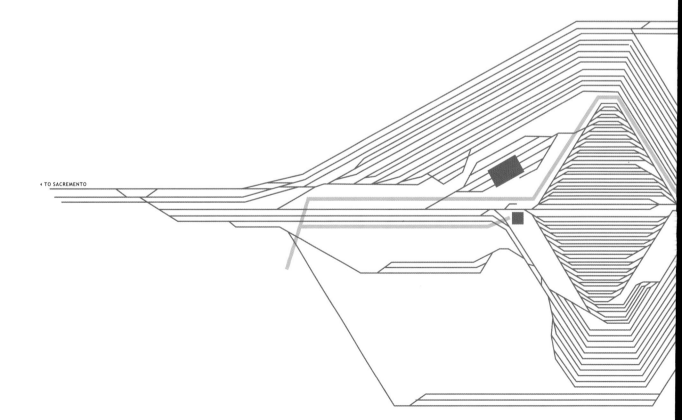

‹ TO SACREMENTO

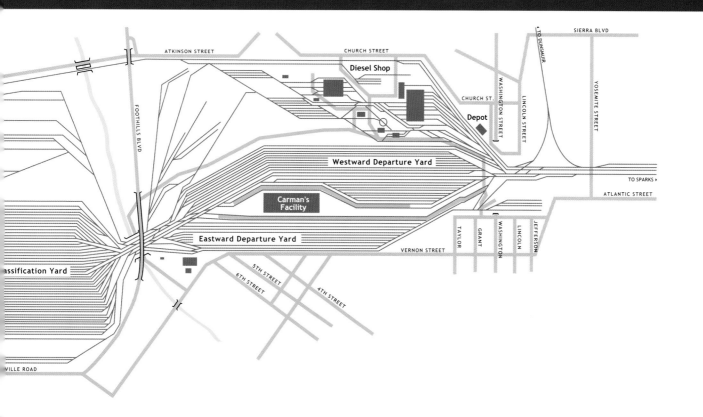

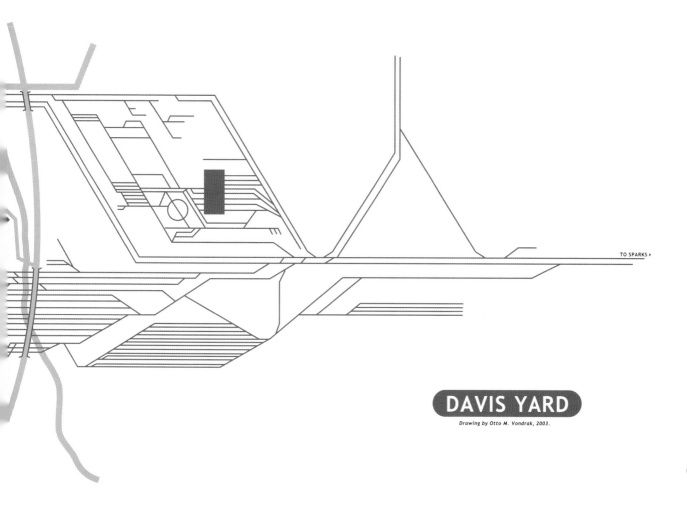

## DAVIS YARD

*Drawing by Otto M. Vondrak, 2003.*

UP owns the redeveloped Roseville Yard, now known as Davis Yard. Here, "Homer Simpson" talks on the radio, awaiting instructions from the yardmaster in 1999.

C41-8W

The 55 classification tracks at Davis are seen to good effect in this view from the hump crest. The many rows of yellow objects adjacent to the tracks are the Dowty retarders, which can both retard and accelerate cars toward a pre-set target velocity.

At the hump of Davis Yard, all car cuts are shown on a big digital scoreboard, to help the pin-pullers in their task of separating cars in the correct places.

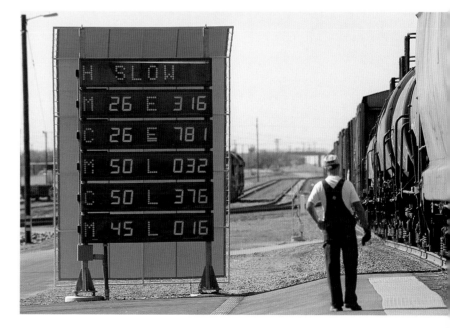

Rio Grande power provides the hump job at Davis, reflecting the ever-changing face of railroad ownership in North America. The hump engines descend into the bowl to pull a track of cars for re-humping.

The departure yard at Davis seems to stretch to infinity. One characteristic of newer yards is the longer track used in both the classification bowl and in the receiving/departure yards. Tracks between 8,000 and 9,000 feet are provided in the new yard.

The telltale wastebasket full of computer printouts means it has been a busy day at the old Davis hump yard.

The view of Davis, then known as Roseville, taken from Foothills Boulevard in 1992 was unobstructed by wire-mesh fencing. This telephoto shot emphasizes one characteristic of the bowl tracks: the short incline toward their exit, which prevents cars rolling straight through the bowl and onto the running tracks. This is particularly clear on the right of this view.

The yard at Pocatello was the first UP hump yard constructed in the postwar period. It was opened in 1947 and lies on the main route to the Pacific Northwest through Idaho. Located at the point where secondary routes from Ogden, Utah, and Montana join the mainline, its importance has fallen significantly in recent years. It ranks as the quietest hump yard on UP, and its classification tracks have been reduced accordingly. It was constructed with a conventional 12-track reception yard, leading to 40 classification tracks and 14 departure roads. By 1996, two fans of classification tracks had been removed, leaving just 28. This change was undoubtedly a reflection of increasing TOFC and COFC traffic as well as a relative reduction in manifest freights.

In March 2002, UP closed the hump at Pocatello. UP estimated that it would cost $10 million to overhaul the aging hump system, operational without much change for more than 50 years. This expense could not be justified, given the shift in terminals to the Pacific Northwest and the new automated facility at Hinkle, which could more than cope with carload traffic in this corner of the country. Most of the bowl tracks at Pocatello will be removed, leaving the remnants of the arrival and departure tracks for any residual traffic.

An early view from the hump crest of Pocatello Yard in the 1950s. Two fans of classification tracks were added later. From expansion to cope with carload traffic came complete closure in 2002. *Union Pacific Museum Collection*

# East Grand Junction Yard—Grand Junction, Colorado

This yard was the only hump facility that the Denver Rio Grande & Western Railroad owned. The merger of DRG&W with SP saw the yard continue its role as an important classification point for traffic over the Tennessee Pass, but UP's purchase of the SP led to drastic changes in the yard's fortunes. In 1996, although some track had been lifted, the yard had 10 arrival tracks and a fully automated hump that led to 30 classification tracks. This is three-quarters of the original number because one fan of 10 had been lifted earlier in the 1990s.

In 1997, however, UP diverted much through traffic away from the Tennessee Pass and consequently decided to close the hump at East Grand Junction Yard. Whether through manifests return to the Tennessee Pass route remains to be seen, but this looks unlikely.

# Bailey Yard—North Platte, Nebraska

Entire books have been written about Bailey (North Platte) Yard and, as it is the largest yard in the world, this is not surprising. Perhaps more surprising is the choice of a windswept Nebraska town as the hub for the entire UP network. The UP rails reached North Platte in 1867, and within 15 years, a roundhouse had been built to accommodate 25 locomotives.

The town is the midpoint between Chicago and Salt Lake City, and it is located on the trails west that were so busy in the mid- and late 1800s. It also served as a useful halfway marker between Omaha and Denver, with good water supplies from the Platte River. The UP chose the area for its base, and the North Platte yard was born. The rest, as they say, is history, and in 1995, the yard was officially recognized in the *Guinness Book of World Records* as the largest marshaling yard in the world.

In terms of number of tracks and sheer size, this is true. In terms of cars dealt with over the hump, it is certainly nowhere near as busy as Hamburg's Maschen Yard in Germany, where up to 11,000 cars can be humped every day.

The first hump classification yard was not built in North Platte until 1948. A single hump yard was built to handle both eastbound and westbound traffic. This yard contained a 1,200-car reception yard, a 1,400-car hump bowl, and a 1,600-car departure yard. This 42-track hump yard replaced a simple flat yard with just 20 tracks that had handled carload traffic through North Platte for more than half a century. In 1968, UP built a second hump, to the south of the 1948 yard, for eastbound traffic. This new yard was much bigger, with 64 classification tracks and a fully automated hump. Meanwhile, the old hump yard was designated to handle westbound traffic.

More changes were still to come in the carload facilities at North Platte. In 1980, the present westbound hump was built on the site of the original 1948 yard. It is interesting to note that the direction for humping westbound traffic is eastbound. This arrangement was necessitated by the strong prevailing westerly winds, which have the power to stop a car dead if humping is undertaken in a westerly direction into the prevailing wind.

Since 1980, expansion has continued apace at North Platte. New tracks and sub yards have been built—not for carload traffic but as a result of increasing intermodal traffic and, of course, Powder River coal traffic. UP started handling Powder River coal traffic in 1984, and now about 50 coal trains a day run on UP metals.

On the north side of the yard complex are 11 run-through tracks for coal and intermodal trains as well as a

This official Union Pacific view shows Bailey Yard's westbound hump yard, built in 1980 with 50 classification tracks. To the right of the classification bowl is the westbound receiving yard. Cars are drawn to a hump lead from here, to be propelled back in the direction they arrived from before being drawn east and placed in the westbound departure yard to the left of the bowl. Further to the left are some of the run-through tracks—mainly occupied with unit coal trains, as can be seen here. *Union Pacific Museum Collection*

seven-track stub yard, which can store up to 450 coal cars. There are plans to expand this yard to 20 tracks and to fit a balloon track at the east end, to allow rapid turnaround of cars back to the Powder River Basin.

The rapid refueling and inspection of locomotives on intermodal and express freight services have been helped enormously by the new "pad" areas in the yard. These are fully equipped service areas, where a train can pull up, refuel, and depart within 30 to 40 minutes, without the need to detach locomotives. The yard has eight such eastbound tracks and seven westbound. The westbound facility lies within the new coal yard, while the eastbound pad is right in the center of the yard complex, between the two hump yards.

In addition to the 300 miles of track, which stretch 7 miles west from North Platte, the yard includes car repair shops and a locomotive repair depot the size of five football fields. The *Guinness Book of Records* lists the yard as

handling 10,000 cars each day. Not all of these pass over the hump—only 3,000 do. The rest represent the coal and intermodal traffic passing through the complex. An average day sees 120 trains passing the yard, 50 to 55 of which are carload. This sort of traffic makes the yard the biggest and perhaps only tourist attraction in North Platte.

Finding the yard is not difficult, as it does dominate the town of North Platte. Turn north off I-80 into North Platte. Several streets in the town cross the yard approaches to the east of the complex. Poplar, North Jeffers, and Willow Streets are all spots to watch the trains on the eastern approaches to the yard. However, Buffalo Bill Avenue is perhaps the best place to the east of the yard, because the departure tracks from the eastbound hump are readily seen from this overpass.

To the west of the yard is a level crossing on Road LC228. This is best reached by crossing to the north of the

An empty boxcar rolls into Bailey's eastbound bowl in 1994. On the right, the engine house can be seen. The westbound bowl lies off to the left in this view.

mainline through North Platte and traveling west along U.S. Highway 30 for 6 miles out of town. A left turn then brings you back to the mainline at the first crossing west of the yard.

One final spot where activity can be observed is the yard's visitor center on the south side of the complex, near the entrance to the engine house. This is reached by driving over the crossing on LC228, heading south to the first left turn, and then driving back into North Platte. The visitor center is on the left and is readily visible at the main entrance to the yard and engine house.

C&NW and UP power lines up in the run-through roads at North Platte in 1994. All are awaiting the call to take their coal empties to the Powder River Basin. Coal traffic through North Platte has increased from virtually nothing to 60 trains each way, every day, over the last 10 years.

The sheer volume of traffic at Bailey Yard leads to inevitable delays. The western approaches to the yard are seen here in 1994. Dash 8 No. 9495 leads another locomotive on an eastbound manifest, while a train of Powder River coal parallels it into the yard. The trains are lined up several miles back, and the headlights of the next pair of arrivals can already be seen in the distance.

Midday heat creates a haze in this 500-millimeter telephoto view taken in May 1994. A pair of Santa Fe engines crosses over the balloon track, which returns westbound motive power over the mainline to the engine house at Bailey Yard. Meanwhile, a pair of C&NW Dash 8s returns an empty unit coal train to the Powder River Basin.

The engine house at Bailey Yard is said to have an area equivalent to five football fields. It is certainly one of the major maintenance facilities on the UP. A whole range of motive power is seen in this view, taken in 1995.

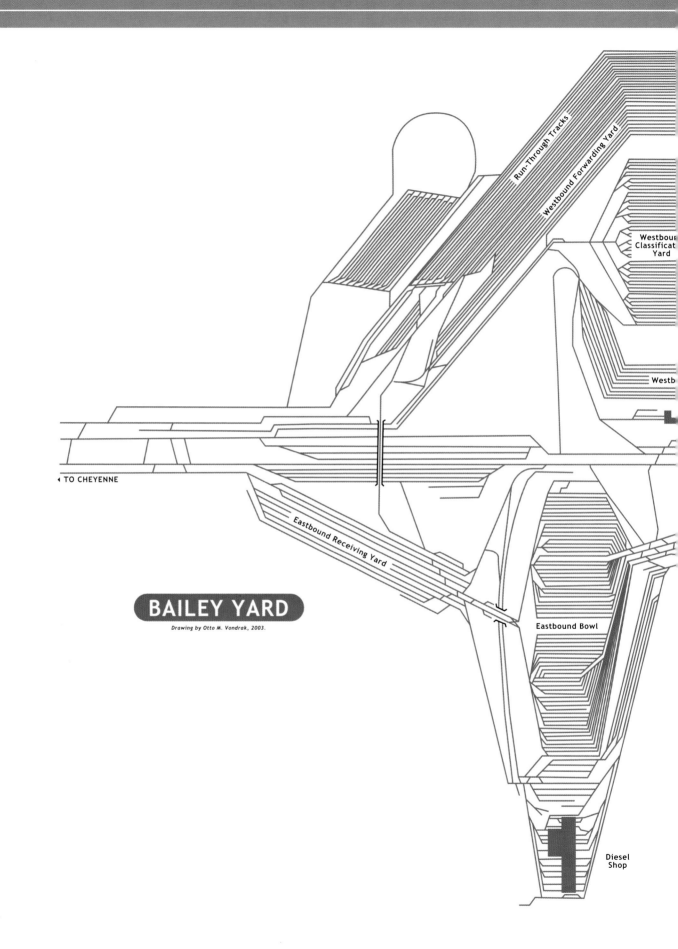

Run-Through Tracks

Westbound Forwarding Yard

Westbour
Classificat
Yard

Westb

**BAILEY YARD**

*Drawing by Otto M. Vondrak, 2003.*

◂ TO CHEYENNE

Eastbound Receiving Yard

Eastbound Bowl

Diesel
Shop

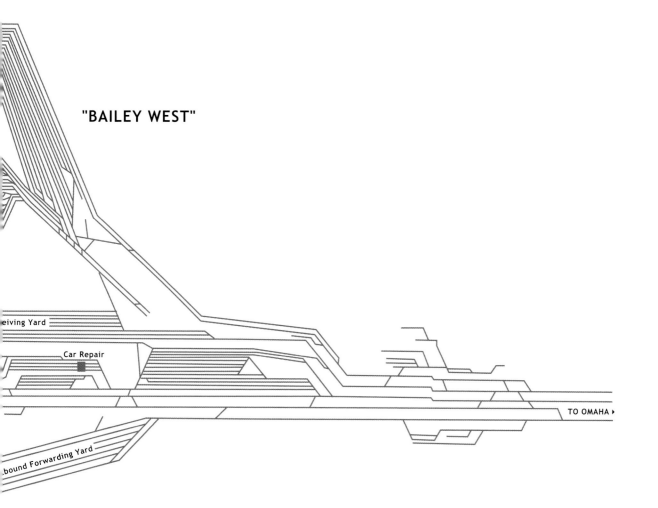

"BAILEY WEST"

Receiving Yard

Car Repair

...bound Forwarding Yard

TO OMAHA ▶

"BAILEY EAST"

UP has several yards in the Kansas City area, which gave it a virtual monopoly on traffic passing through this gateway in the early years of railroads. Not until ATSF arrived in town was this monopoly broken. As for UP, it built two large flat-switched yards to the west of the city, at 18th Street and Armstrong. Here, a host of eastern railroads, including Wabash, Chicago Burlington & Quincy, Gulf Mobile & Ohio, Milwaukee, Chicago & North Western, and Missouri Pacific interchanged traffic with UP.

The modern-day UP has absorbed the Missouri Pacific, and as a result, the major UP yard in Kansas City today is no longer to the west of town but to the east, at Neff Yard. This yard was built by the Missouri Pacific back in the 1950s and had both a westbound and an eastbound hump. The westbound half of the yard has been removed, with the land given over to intermodal traffic. This used to consist of 11 arrival tracks, 30 classification roads, and 11 departure tracks. In addition, 10 run-through tracks for unit trains are still partly in use.

The eastbound classification yard was larger and benefited from a total rebuild in the 1980s. It is used today as the main location for classifying cars in Kansas City. Eighteen arrival roads lead to 40 classification tracks and then 12 departure tracks, which are laid out along the arrival tracks.

Today the hump classifies 1,500 cars per day. The terminal area handles 5,000 cars per day, the majority as run-through cars on unit and intermodal trains. The yard is blessed with an excellent observation point in the Manchester Chouteau Trafficway, which crosses the yard area right over the eastbound hump. It is a lightly trafficked road and provides excellent views of the hump, classification tracks, and departure area.

Also clearly visible from Manchester Trafficway are the departure tracks for Neff hump yard. Here, five UP units have just run from the small engine house at the east end of the complex and are about to head south with a long manifest, made up mainly of grain cars. UP 6209 arrives with a solitary car with an out-of-gauge iron casting that had been photographed leaving 18th Street Yard just an hour earlier (see page 78).

Looking west off the Manchester Trafficway, the takeover by intermodal traffic is evident. The vacant land behind the intermodal cars is all that remains of the westbound classification tracks. Just a few roads are used for run-through grain trains and car storage, which can be seen beyond the waste ground. Four UP units get ready to head east to Chicago with a TOFC service, which they will build from the short tracks at Neff.

The view east from Manchester Trafficway gives an excellent appreciation of the Neff classification bowl and its 40 tracks. In 1995, grain cars roll into the far right track.

# 18ᵗʰ Street Yard—Kansas City, Kansas

The UP yards to the west of town are a source of some confusion. There were two major yards, the most westerly called 18th Street Yard and the one nearer town called Armstrong Yard. In the 1970s and 1980s, Armstrong Yard was by far the more important for manifest and carload traffic. It boasted 50 tracks and was also the location of UP's main one-spot car repair shop and the engine house. However, this yard has largely been converted to intermodal traffic.

The switching of manifest traffic has been transferred to 18th Street Yard, which is very busy, as the photograph shows. Thirty fairly lengthy tracks suffice for carload switching. These are easy to observe from 18th Street itself, which spans the eastern end of the yard as well as the UP mainline into Kansas City and the remains of the old SP Armourdale Yard.

UP 6209 prepares to leave the 18th Street Yard with an iron casting. Cars are switched from both the east and west ends of the yard. This view from the 18th Street overpass gives an excellent panorama of the yard as well as the adjacent mainline and ex-SP yards.

The massive yard at Gateway is now wholly owned by the UP. It was built by the Alton and Southern Railroad, a belt railroad serving the St. Louis area. In 1968, the Missouri Pacific (MoPac) and Chicago & North Western (C&NW) purchased the Alton Railroad. The Cotton Belt Railroad purchased C&NW's share of ownership in 1973. UP took over MoPac in 1982 and SP in 1996. UP, therefore, is sole owner of the Alton and Southern and also its massive Gateway Yard.

The yard itself has a most unusual layout, with all tracks lying parallel to one another. Trains are propelled over the hump with the engines pushing in an easterly direction as the cars move around a large balloon track and into the classification yard in a westerly direction. The photos should make this clear. First, 10 arrival tracks feed

a 66-track classification bowl, which in turn leads around another balloon to seven departure roads. During a visit in 1999, the hump was handling 800 cars per shift, or 2,400 per day, making Gateway one of the busiest yards on the UP when measured by individual cars handled.

Unfortunately, the yard is one of the most inaccessible in the United States, with no public places from which to view action. The official entrance to the yard is on 22nd Street in East St. Louis, which is off Bond Street. There are tracks and lanes around the yard perimeter, and the southern side of the railroad land is bordered by the Sauget Indian Parkway. Between this and Gateway are the tracks of the Illinois Central yard and also the old Southern yard. The area is also fairly rough, and hanging around outside the safety of railroad land is not advisable.

The view from the hump tower at Gateway offers the city of St. Louis in the background and the symbolic Gateway Arch, on the other side of the Mississippi River. The dual hump leads to eleven fans of tracks, six on the south side and five on the north. Although the yard looks massive, several yards have larger classification fans, including Elkhart, Toronto, and Montreal.

## Manifest Departures from Gateway Yard on a Typical Day in 1999

| TIME | TRAIN NUMBER | TO |
|---|---|---|
| 01.00 | 135 | Clearing Yard |
| 01.00 | 305 | St. Louis industries |
| 02.00 | 196 | Nashville |
| 02.00 | 331 | Englewood Yard |
| 03.00 | 312 | St. Louis industries |
| 04.00 | 210 | Avon Yard, Selkirk Yard |
| 04.00 | 147 | Rose Lake local |
| 06.00 | 302 | Madison Yard |
| 06.00 | 204 | Livonia |
| 07.00 | 333 | Springfield, Illinois, Yard |
| 09.00 | 327 | Kansas City |
| 11.00 | 121 | Pine Bluff Yard |
| 12.00 | 310 | St. Louis industries |
| 14.00 | 323 | Pine Bluff Yard |
| 14.30 | 324 | Bailey (North Platte) Yard |
| 15.00 | 315 | Cincinnati |
| 17.00 | 144 | Arlington, Texas |
| 18.00 | 200 | North Little Rock Yard |
| 18.00 | 316 | Proviso Yard, Battle Creek |
| 19.00 | 371 | Elkhart Yard, Conway Yard, and Decatur Yard |
| 19.00 | 311 | St. Louis industries |
| 23.00 | 321 | Kansas City |

Footnote: On the day described above, the yard at Gateway had 155 cars for Englewood, with one train in the departure yard, limited to 80 cars. Because UP did not double up departure roads to make longer trains, an extra service ran to Englewood that day. In addition to the trains listed above, several extra services always ran from Gateway.

Crewmembers on an Alton & Southern switcher await their orders.

Three Alton & Southern yard slugs make their way into the reception yard, where they will propel another manifest over the hump.

# Centennial Yard—Fort Worth, Texas

Centennial Yard in Fort Worth was originally constructed in 1971 as a modern hump yard by the Texas & Pacific Railroad. Subsequent takeover by first the Missouri Pacific and then UP in 1982 makes it one of UP's assets. Texas & Pacific built it as a twin-track hump, and MoPac rebuilt it in 1978. The yard has 8 arrival tracks, 44 classification tracks, and 12 departure tracks. During my visit in 1998, it was handling 1,200 to 1,500 cars per day over the hump. One other interesting facet is that a manifest departure from Fort Worth during my visit arrived at its destination in Tulsa 32 hours later. However, the road journey is little more than six hours!

Access to the yard is not bad. From I-30 heading east, take the Rosedale Street exit (this is to the west of downtown by about 3 miles). From Rosedale, turn right (south) on Hulen. After 800 yards, Hulen spans the hump area of the yard on a viaduct. Also, Rosedale Street swings over the eastern end of the yard on another viaduct.

The view from the hump tower at Centennial Yard emphasizes the high-tech side of modern manifest marshaling. Gone are the polished metal switches, replaced by modern computer monitors.

Cars roll in quick succession into the 44 classification tracks at Centennial Yard. The more sophisticated the computer technology, the shorter the headway between cars, and the larger among of cars that can be humped in a given time.

# Englewood Yard—Houston, Texas

Cars roll in quick succession into the classification tracks at Englewood. Three separate cars can be seen in the retarder area at one time.

Houston is a complex railway terminal, where 120 trains converge on the city every day from 12 different routes. With UP having taken over first the Missouri Pacific and then SP, the two major yards in the city, at Settegast and Englewood, now belong to UP. Houston also is the center for the nadir of recent UP history—the infamous autumn 1997 meltdown. In short, UP took over the SP and instituted several changes in operations, aimed at concentrating as much carload traffic as possible on the massive SP hump yard at Englewood. The yard seized up, and with it most of the UP.

The SP built Englewood in 1954, at a cost of $7.6 million. With 64 classification tracks and capacity to hold 7,179 cars within the yard tracks, it was the SP's biggest yard. It also has 6 east reception roads and another 12 reception roads wrapped around the north and south sides of the classification bowl. It has nine departure tracks: four on the north side of the bowl and five on the south side.

During my visit in 1998, the yard was classifying 1,500 cars per day over the hump, and SP staff said that anything over 1,700 cars per day would cause the yard to seize up. In 1979, just such a problem had occurred. To rescue the yard

from complete chaos, the SP removed 1,500 cars from the yard and parked them on a little-used branchline. It is therefore surprising, with such a history, that the UP decided to scale down classification at secondary yards around Houston and pour more work into Englewood. Attempts to divert work handled by Strang Yard to Englewood led to the complete meltdown of UP freight services in October 1997.

Three units are one of the hump "tricks" at Englewood and are seen here pulling cars out of the arrival tracks to the south of the classification bowl. The yard has two pullback tracks alongside its six east reception tracks. The engines will pull their cars back into one of these tracks before changing direction to hump their cars into the bowl.

Strang is a small hump yard in the port area of Houston, 25 miles east of downtown. It was amazingly efficient with only 13 classification tracks, and with four arrival and departure roads classifying 900 cars per day in 1997. The yard handled three long-distance arrivals and four long-distance departures daily, and was cleared twice every 24 hours. Each classification track was equipped with its own air-power retarder, with a range of target speeds for cars from 3 to 9 miles per hour.

Trains departed from there to Memphis, Livonia, and St. Louis. In addition, 11 industry and dock jobs shuttled to and from the yard, handling the complex chemical and dock traffic generated by the port of Houston's south side.

The yard had only seven jobs each day in the 1970s, when it first opened. The petrochemical industry in the area had expanded so much that by the time of my visit in 1998, there were 32 jobs per day. With the yard's importance fully recognized after the aforementioned meltdown of October 1997, the UP planned to expand the classification bowl to 14 tracks and to increase arrival and departure roads from four to eight.

The small bowl at Strang is seen here from the control tower.

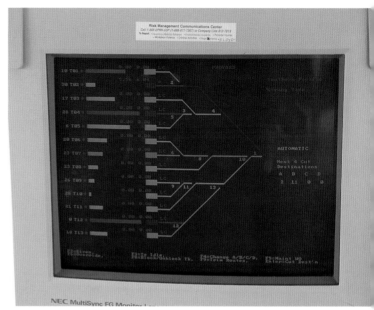

For all its apparent insignificance, Strang Yard is pivotal to the smooth running of Houston's railroads. It is equipped with the most modern yard technology and keeps nearly 1,000 cars a day away from Houston's congested center.

Ex-C&NW and SP power heads a string of nearly 100 cars bound for St. Louis. The train is about to leave the four arrival/departure tracks at Strang.

A pair of SP yard switchers prepare to hump shunt at Strang.

The UP also owns a large flat yard in Houston, at Settegast, which has 38 classification tracks, with seven arrival and seven departure roads. The UP has divided tasks in its Houston yards. Settegast handles most long-distance departures to the northern and eastern United States, with 17 manifest departures each day toward Fort Worth, North Little Rock, and Livonia. In contrast, Englewood handles most local industrial traffic in the Houston area and dispatches trains toward Brownsville and San Antonio. Strang continues to handle chemical traffic and to take the pressure off the city center yards, as do other, smaller yards at Dayton and Spring.

Access to Houston's yards is generally difficult. Traveling east on Highway 610, there is an excellent bridge over the east end of Englewood Yard, but one cannot stop. Exit from 610 onto I-90 at North Wayside and go right on Wallisville Road to find the entrance to the yard. Unfortunately, views of the yard from public places are difficult to find.

The same is true for Settegast Yard, which lies 1 mile due north of the Englewood hump. As for Strang Yard, follow Route 225, called La Porte Freeway, for 20 miles east of Houston, take the exit for Strang, and look for the sign illustrated in this section. To be honest, I cannot remember exactly how I got to the yard, but it wasn't difficult to find!

# Livonia Yard—Livonia, Louisiana

Livonia Yard is unique in modern railroad history, in that it is completely new, built on a greenfield site in Louisiana. The yard was needed because of the increase in petrochemical traffic along the coast between New Orleans and Houston, which brought large increases in carload traffic for the UP. The yard lies 2 miles south of the township of Livonia and was constructed using the Dowty retarder system.

Dowty retarders were invented in England and were first used on a trial basis in the late 1950s in a small yard at Goodmayes, in Essex. The advantage of these small rheostatic retarders is that they allow for more controlled retardation than can be achieved with the traditional rail brakes used in most hump yards. The Dowty system was used in three large yards in England and has since been successfully employed in the Villach and Wien Kledering yards in Austria. Its most recent employment is in the Livonia (Louisiana) and Roseville (northern California) yards, where the UP has used the retarders for its new classification yards. Even the Chinese appear to have used the system at yards around Shenyang, although it is not clear whether this was with permission.

The dash-pots of the Dowty retarders are prominent in this view of the locomotives that arrived with a train of 130 cars from Little Rock. Another unusual feature of Livonia Yard is that the road power on arriving trains may be used to propel a train over the hump before retiring to the engine house for refueling and servicing.

Since construction in 1995, the yard has been enlarged. It now has a seven-track receiving yard and a seven-track departure yard, with a pair of pullback tracks for the hump. The classification bowl contains 35 roads that are longer than in older yards and can hold 60 to 80 cars each. What the yard lacks in grandeur, compared to older yards such as Englewood, it exceeds in efficiency. An amazing number of cars—3,000—are classified each day at Livonia, nearly twice as many as in Englewood.

Two SD40s leave the yard at Livonia with a train for Avondale Yard in New Orleans.

The hump crest in a Dowty yard is much lower than in traditional hump yards. The Dowty retarders may both retard and accelerate a car to reach its target velocity. The imperative for a high-speed exit from the hump is therefore not the same as with traditional yards. This view, taken in 1998, shows the classification bowl at Livonia.

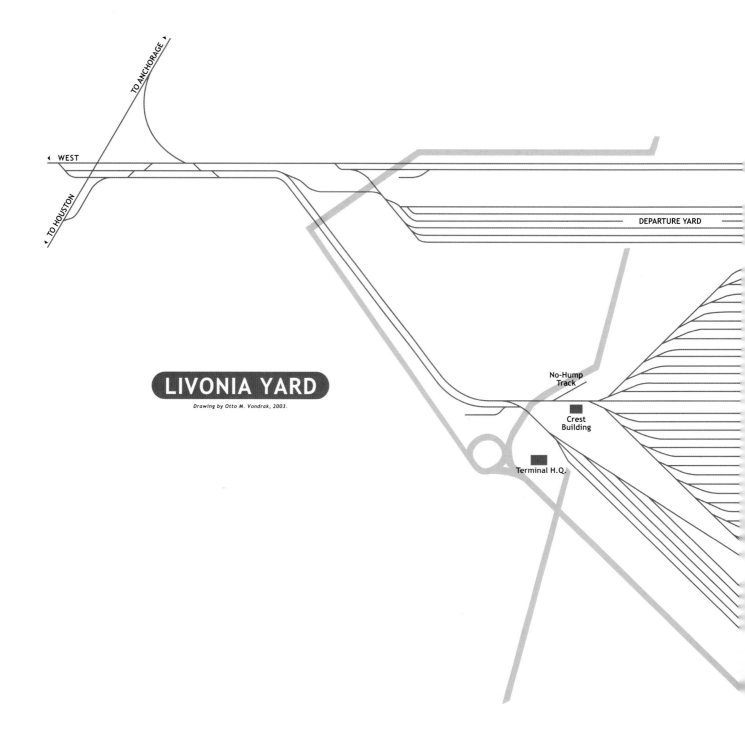

TO ANCHORAGE

WEST

TO HOUSTON

DEPARTURE YARD

# LIVONIA YARD

*Drawing by Otto M. Vondrak, 2003.*

No-Hump
Track

Crest
Building

Terminal H.Q.

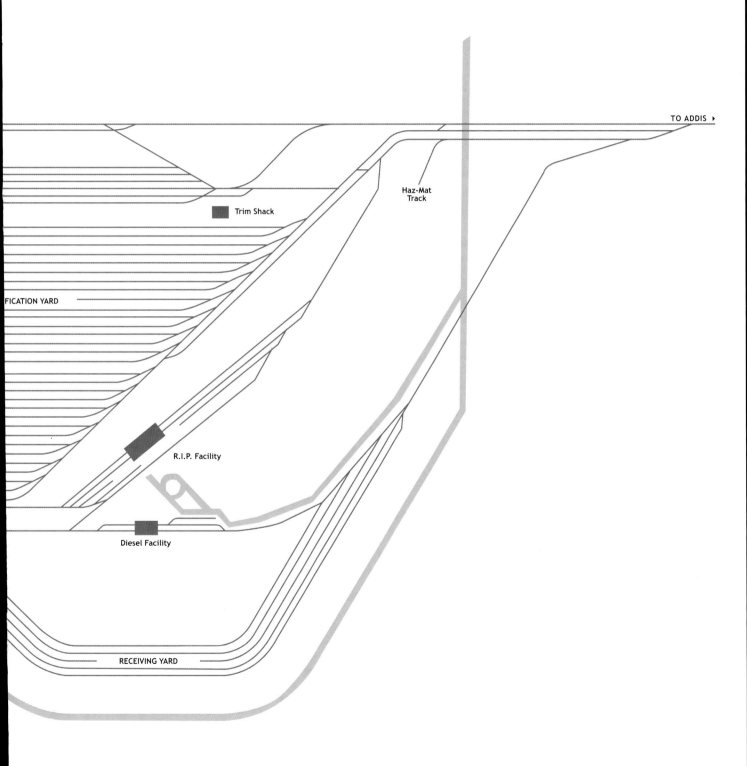

TO ADDIS ▸

Haz-Mat
Track

Trim Shack

FICATION YARD

R.I.P. Facility

Diesel Facility

RECEIVING YARD

North Little Rock Yard opened in 1961, built by the Missouri Pacific at a cost of $8.4 million. The yard was the hub of MoPac freight operations and, when opened, had 40 classification tracks and room for 4,500 cars. The yard is now an integral part of the UP. Since the merger with SP and the problems that followed, North Little Rock has classified almost exclusively northbound manifest traffic. Neighboring Pine Bluff handles the southbound traffic.

The yard of today is larger than when originally constructed. Eight reception tracks lead to the hump and 64 classification roads. There are 12 departure tracks, and the complex handles more than 60 trains every day. On the day of my visit in 1998, 2,300 cars had been over the hump in the previous 24 hours. The yard staff quoted the maximum capacity of the facility as 2,500 cars per day. The potential for expansion and more run-through tracks may well be exploited, because spare land is adjacent to the yard.

Access to the yard is poor. Main Street in North Little Rock crosses the western approaches to the yard and gives a view over the Jenks locomotive shops, but there are no views of the yard. I-30 does cross the western end of the yard, but it isn't possible to stop there. Similarly, I-40 crosses the eastern end of the complex. There is access to the eastern end of the yard on West Bethany Road, off Route 161, but this spot is more for observation than photography.

Boxcars roll down the hump into the class bowl at North Little Rock in 1998.

UP yard goats with extra power draw cars out of the bowl at North Little Rock for re-humping.

This photograph mounted on the wall of the main yard office gives an excellent impression of the size of the North Little Rock facility.

It's lunchtime for the UP switchers imported to work the hump at Pine Bluff.

Pine Bluff was a Cotton Belt yard, built in 1958. With the merger of UP and SP, Pine Bluff has become a partner yard with the larger North Little Rock facility. It handles southbound traffic along the Arkansas corridor, while North Little Rock handles northbound. The yard has 41 classification tracks, six arrival roads and eight departure roads. In 1998, it was handling 1,500 cars per 24 hours over the hump.

The yard lies northeast of Pine Bluff. To get to it, exit U.S. Highway 65 eastbound at Texas Street and take the first left onto Second Avenue, which continues east as Port Road. After 2 miles, Port Road runs along the entire northern border of the yard, giving excellent views of activity.

A long string of cars is propelled over the hump with the retarders in the raised, or off, position. With long cuts of cars, hump shunting effectively becomes old-fashioned flat-switching in a yard like Pine Bluff.

Riding the cars the old-fashioned way.

After the merger of Chicago & North Western into the mighty UP in 1995, UP obtained a direct route to the Windy City from the west and also a suitably sized classification yard for all its Chicago-bound traffic—that yard is Proviso. When it opened in 1929, the new Proviso Yard was the largest in the world. It was built on swampland, and 1,250 acres of land were prepared with landfill, using slag from the many Chicago steel mills. The site chosen had an unusual "L" shape, with the long limb stretching 5.5 miles east to west. The sheer size of the area can be gauged by the fact that it contained 260 miles of track, which could accommodate 26,000 cars.

The heart of the yard was the hump classification part of the facility, which is still largely unchanged. Because of the Depression of the 1930s, the yard was not used to its full capacity until World War II. During the 1940s, between 7,000 and 8,000 cars were classified daily. Other areas of the yard included a 21-acre freight transfer house for less than carload goods, an icing plant for refrigerator cars, and a 58-stall roundhouse (later replaced by the big diesel house that exists today).

In the 1940s, there were an average of 128 arrivals and departures daily. In the 1950s, bigger cars with longer wheelbases meant that hump capacity was significantly

Yard pilot No. 6657 trims a solitary car that has failed to make it through the retarders correctly. The scene is viewed from the Proviso Yard hump control tower, with the classification bowl stretching away into the background. The Mannheim Street Bridge can just be made out in the distance.

The C&NW engine house at Proviso is photographed from the Mannheim Street Bridge on a dreary day in May 1995.

less (as measured by cars classified per day), and a second approach to the twin hump was built. The classification bowl was also expanded, from 59 tracks to 66.

During a visit in 1995, Proviso still classified 750 cars every shift over the hump, totaling over 2,000 every day. Work at the yard is split between carload and container trains, and the Global II facility, built on the site of the old yard's number 6, 7, and 8 tracks, makes more than 200,000 container lifts per year. The number of trains the yard generates is less than 50 years ago, but the trains are generally heavier. Thirty manifests depart to the west and north as well, and the yard sees up to 10 run-through manifests. The yard provides work for 1,200 people, if jobs in the engine house are counted.

Proviso Yard lies a couple of miles south of O'Hare International Airport, and if the approach to Chicago is favorable, flyers can get an excellent view of the yard's layout. It is unusual in that it has a 90 degree bend in the middle, with the reception yard lying north to south and the classification bowl laid out from west to east.

Several roads pass under the yard, most notably North Avenue and Lake Street, both of which pass under the main lead from the 30 reception roads into the 66-track classification bowl. There are also gates into the yard here, for those with permission to access the premises. For an overview of the yard, the only option is Mannheim Road, which stretches for nearly 400 yards across the departure yards. The western view from the bridge includes the engine house.

Cars roll over the hump at 15-second intervals. The IHB gondola loaded with steel will need the strongest retarder setting to bring its heavy load to rest appropriately.

The hump crest at Proviso is shown here with the dual-hump lead curving away to the right. For such a large classification yard, the small, two-story hump tower is a bit of a disappointment.

The Canadian National (CN) railroad was founded in 1919, when the Canadian government rescued three private companies in financial trouble. CN remained a state-run railroad until 1995, when it was privatized. At the start of the 1990s, CN owned five active hump yards, in Moncton, Montreal, Toronto, Winnipeg, and Edmonton. Three of these are some of the biggest in North America and were all built at the same time, in the early 1960s: Taschereau (Montreal), MacMillan (Toronto), and Symington (Winnipeg). In 1994, the yard at Moncton closed its hump and downsized considerably, leaving CN with just four home-built yards.

Canadian National is the larger of the two Canadian Railroads and, like its smaller sister, Canadian Pacific, makes significant incursions into the United States. Since 1971, the Grand Trunk Western Railroad (GTW) has been part of CN, giving access as far south as Cincinnati and connecting CN to Detroit. GTW owned just one major hump yard at Flat Rock, to the south of Detroit, but the hump closed in 1996. In 1998, CN purchased Illinois Central. While this added more than 2,600 miles to its network, no more hump yards were added to the railroad.

Of previous Illinois Central yards, only those at Markham, south of Chicago, and East St. Louis were hump-operated. The other major yards in Memphis and New Orleans always have been flat-switched. In 2003, the yard at East St. Louis lies virtually derelict. Markham is a hive of activity for container traffic, with both humps demolished and much of the vast acreage turned over to the container revolution. This leaves the CN of 2003 with more than 18,000 route miles, but just four active hump yards.

Cars roll down the hump at Taschereau. The train being classified can be seen disappearing around the balloon track on the right. The hump had two tracks that allowed simultaneous classification of two arrivals. More often, however, one train was humped at a time, with a second string of cars propelled up to the hump crest on the vacant line. This reduced the gap between humping to an absolute minimum. The rust-brown metal plate on the left hump track is the weight bridge, used to weigh cars as part of the calculation to ensure correct speed into the yard bowl.

This remarkable yard is a product of the 1960s building program on CN, along with MacMillan and Symington yards. It was opened in 1961 at a cost of $28.5 million and is very much a product of the philosophy that "bigger is better." Indeed, Taschereau has the largest single fan of classification tracks in North America, with 81 radiating from the primary hump.

The confines of suburban west Montreal have led to a layout not dissimilar to Gateway Yard in St. Louis, where reception and departure tracks lie parallel to the main classification bowl. Cars to be sorted over the hump are propelled around a large, three-track balloon at the north of the complex. The yard has a double hump, which in 1996 was still classifying 1,500 cars every day. The two central fans of the main classification bowl are relatively short and led to a secondary hump, which in turn led to a 37-track secondary classification bowl. This was used to reclassify local traffic but was closed in 1994.

Also in 1994, Moncton Yard in eastern Canada closed its hump, as carload traffic declined and less marshaling of freight trains was needed. It had been a large yard, opened in 1960, with room for more than 5,000 cars on its tracks. The hump led to a 40-track bowl, but it has now been razed. Taschereau was also home to a large engine house, but this, too, closed in 1996, and all heavy repairs of the CN diesels in the east were moved to MacMillan.

Access to the yard at Taschereau is one of the most difficult in North America. The yard is 9.3 miles southwest of the city center, in the area of town called Côte-St. Luc, three-quarters of the way to the old international airport at Dorval.

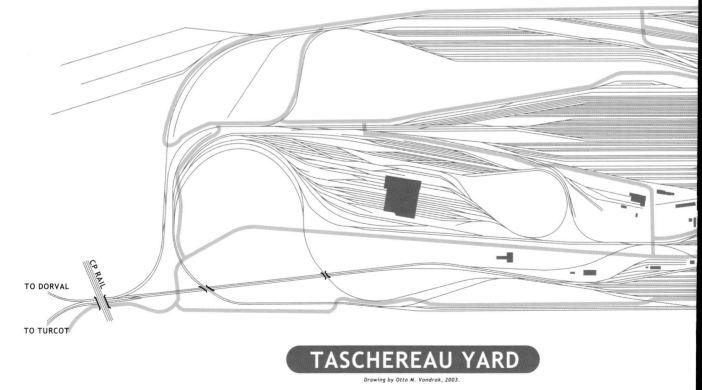

TO DORVAL

CP RAIL

TO TURCOT

TASCHEREAU YARD

*Drawing by Otto M. Vondrak, 2003.*

A solitary chemical car rolls into the westernmost fan in the classification bowl at Taschereau in October 1996.

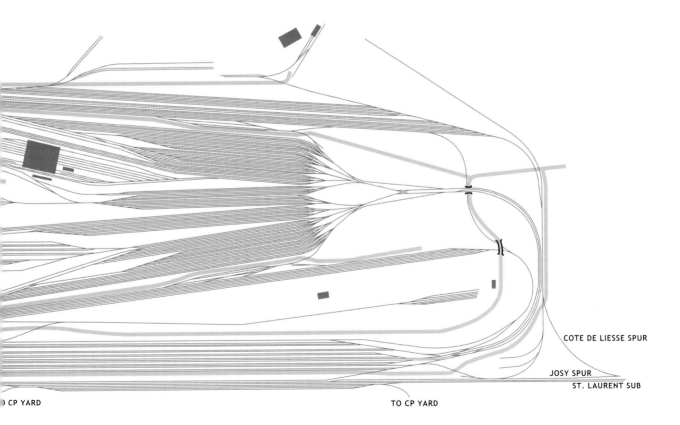

COTE DE LIESSE SPUR

JOSY SPUR

ST. LAURENT SUB

CP YARD

TO CP YARD

This wonderful CN publicity photo shows the world's largest classification bowl to excellent effect. *Canadian National*

Toronto's MacMillan Yard is the largest on CN and one of the largest in North America. It opened in 1965 at a cost of $44 million and is 12.4 miles north of Toronto's city center. The yard is unusual in that it is laid out like the old-time passenger grand termini, as a dead-end facility. Trains arrive from the CN York Sub to the south of the complex via the 21 arrival roads that run alongside the two classification yards. Trains are then drawn north onto one of two stub-end tracks before being propelled onto the main hump. Like Taschereau, the yard has a double-track primary hump bowl, which at MacMillan has 72 tracks. The center tracks in the bowl lead to a secondary hump, which has its own 50-track bowl where local traffic is classified.

During my visit in 1996, the yard classified 2,000 cars every day over the main hump. A study of the logs revealed 999 manifest departures during September 1996, an average of 33 trains per day. The yard was working at capacity and had interesting plans to increase the throughput. The capacity of 2,000 cars per day was based on an approach speed of 1.7 miles per hour. By upgrading the computer hardware and using new software, exactly the same tracks and hump could be used with an approach speed of 2.3

miles per hour. This may not seem like a major advance, and it certainly did not involve any major earthworks or external changes at the yard. It did, however, mean that the daily capacity of the hump could be increased to 2,600 cars per 24 hours, a massive 30 percent increase in throughput.

The secondary hump handled 350 cars per shift, or 1,000 per day, and was manually operated using retarders controlled by the yardmaster. This, too, was being automated, to allow more cars to be classified. In addition to changes in the yard, the nearby engine house was taking on more work in 1996, as the houses at Taschereau and Moncton in the east had closed, leaving just MacMillan, Symington, and Walker as the three major maintenance facilities on CN. This of course excludes the GTW maintenance facility in Battle Creek and the IC facilities taken over by CN as a result of the merger in 1998.

Access to the yard is in stark contrast to Taschereau. Highway 7, which runs across the north of greater Toronto, passes over the southern exit from the yard and offers several excellent photo positions and a guaranteed view of every arrival and departure from the complex.

A CN boxcar rolls down the primary hump at MacMillan in October 1996. The 72 classification tracks can be seen stretched out across the horizon.

Two safety-cab GP40-2 engines pull their arrival out of the MacMillan arrival yard north onto the primary hump approach tracks. This view was taken from the hump tower during an official visit arranged with CN.

The secondary hump at MacMillan is much smaller than the primary. The yardmaster manually controls the retarders in the tower on the right. During 1996, plans were well underway for automating this hump.

The engine house at MacMillan is the largest on CN, with responsibility for more than 500 diesels. In 1995, the facility had just 199 units based there, but in 1996 it took over approximately 500 from Taschereau and 150 from Moncton Yard in New Brunswick. This made it by far the largest workshop on CN. Here, GP40-2 No. 9619, an ex-Taschereau engine, awaits repairs in the engine house.

One of Macmillan's GP9 switchers, No. 7221, draws cars south out of the secondary yard. The engine is viewed from the Highway 7 overpass in 1996.

Cars from the dead-end drawback tracks are seen on the primary hump crest at MacMillan.

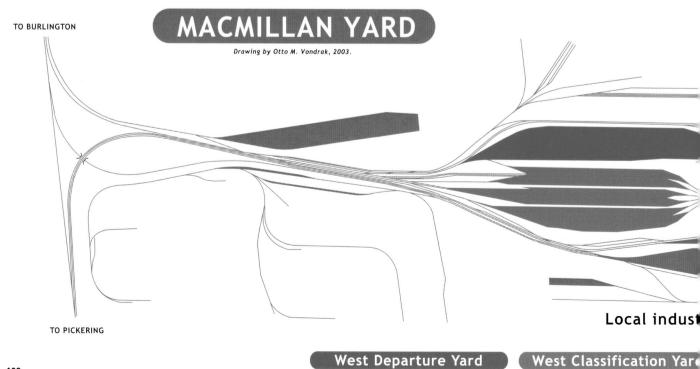

Cars of all shapes and sizes fill the secondary bowl at MacMillan Yard in October 1996. The hump for the bowl can just be seen in the distance. This view is also taken from the Highway 7 overpass.

**Shops**

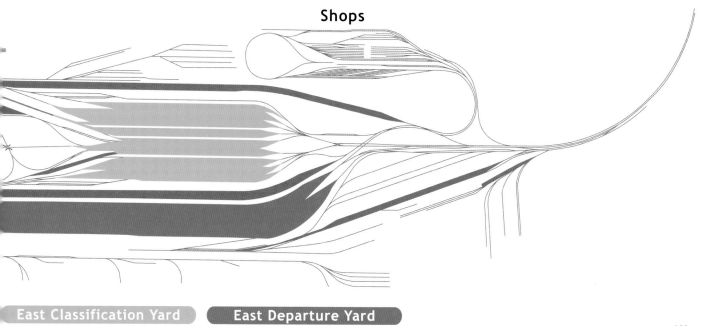

East Classification Yard    East Departure Yard

# Symington Yard—Winnipeg, Manitoba

Symington Yard lies on the eastern outskirts of Winnipeg. It opened in 1962, at a cost of $24 million, and provided work for 2,000 employees. It has a traditional layout, with arrival and departure tracks alongside a 70-track classification bowl. It originally had just 63 classification tracks, but subsequent traffic levels have justified the addition of a new balloon, with 7 more tracks. Cars are drawn out of the arrival yard before being propelled back over the hump. The hump handles a maximum of 600 cars per eight-hour shift. There are 20 trains each day, mostly from local branchlines, with just a handful of long-haul manifests each day to the expected destinations of MacMillan, Edmonton, and Clearing.

This yard's biggest challenge is the winter, when temperatures drop to minus 40 degrees, not including the wind-chill factor. These conditions complicate much of the hump operation.

The yard is east of Winnipeg and is easy to find. Head south from town on Route 52, then take a left fork onto Route 150 (called St. Anne's Road). After about two-thirds of a mile, turn left onto Route 135 (called Fermor Avenue) and follow this for 3 miles until it crosses the east end of Symington Yard, the ideal position from which to photograph the hump.

This view from the hump tower at Symington, taken in April 1998, shows a string of cars being propelled over the hump, while the Chicago train waits on the left. The lights of an approaching manifest can just be seen on the horizon.

This busy view from Fermor Avenue gives a good impression of the hump at Symington Yard. A string of cars is propelled over the hump by a pair of GP38 yard goats, while another pair has just finished humping its train. On the right, SD50 No. 5450, based in Edmonton, Alberta, heads a 92-car consist bound for Chicago Clearing via Fort Frances, Ontario, and Duluth, Minnesota.

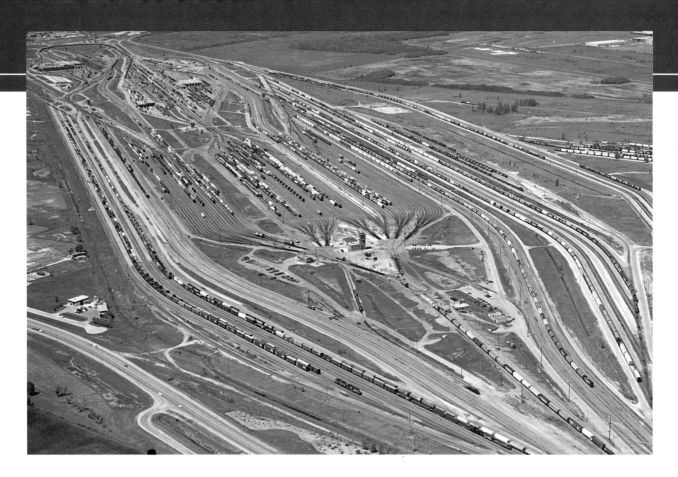

This excellent CN publicity shot shows the yard from the air on a splendidly clear day. The classification bowl fills the center of the view, with room for more tracks should the need arise. This is not unusual and is most evident at Bellevue Yard, the NS facility in Ohio, where just half the bowl has actually been built. *Canadian National*

The sun sets as the yardmaster keeps tabs on things in the Symington hump tower. *Canadian National*

The smallest operational hump yard on CN is in Edmonton. The yard comprises a 34-track classification bowl, which handled up to 400 cars per shift in 1998. When I spoke with the yardmaster during my visit in 1998, she informed me that there were 2,896 cars within the Walker terminal area. Most of these were part of unit trains of coal or grain, which did not need classifying.

The yard itself lies to the north of the city and on the northern edge of the Edmonton Municipal Airport. Highway 16, which is a dual highway, lies along the southern border of the yard and along the northern edge of 127th Avenue. Glimpses of the yard are possible from both of these locations, but there are no good spots for observation. Entry into the yard itself is from the 87th Street underpass, which runs south from 127th Avenue to a junction with Highway 16, beneath the eastern neck of the yard area.

Because winters can be harsh in northern Alberta, the retarders for Walker's 34-track class yard are protected by snow shields.

The master retarder has its own snow shed at Walker. Cars are seen rolling through it in April 1998.

While equal opportunities apparently exist for most jobs, railroading is still male-dominated. The hump tower at Walker was the only place I met a female yard employee in my 14 years of travels to more than 100 yards.

The only hump yard on lines purchased from the GTW was at Flat Rock, south of Detroit. GTW also has major flat-switched yards at Lansing, Detroit, and Battle Creek. The latter is also the site of the main GTW engine house and repair shops.

The yard at Flat Rock was a classic hump facility. In 1996, the retarders needed renewing, but the cost could not be justified. The hump and retarders were therefore removed in 1996, and classification tracks 1 and 36 were also lifted. This left a 34-track bowl, which was flat-switched from both ends. The throughput at the yard was down to less than 600 cars per day when I visited in 2002.

The yard is south of Detroit in Flat Rock and lies in open countryside to the east of the city's center. Traveling north on I-75, take the Gibraltar Road exit just after the highway has split with Route 85. Turn left toward Flat Rock and then right on Cahill Road, after just over a mile. This meets Vreeland Road at a T-junction. Turn left on Vreeland Road, follow the bridge over the old hump approach, then turn left onto Hall Road. There is a rail crossing at the east end of the yard, near the engine servicing point. The countryside is not built up, and access around the yard is fairly easy.

The view from the old hump tower at Flat Rock shows clearly the classical bowl layout of the erstwhile hump facility.

Battle Creek, Michigan, is home for 280 GTW engines, but Flat Rock has a small refueling facility, seen here in the evening sun of October 2002.

The Illinois Central (IC) no longer has any hump yards but was in many ways a front-runner in hump yard construction. The first all-electric retarders were installed in the IC yard in East St. Louis. This yard only had a small 24-track bowl but continued as a hump yard until it was sold to the Gateway Western Railroad in 1986. The hump is no longer used and is partially dismantled, as my 1999 picture shows. IC also had a large hump yard in Memphis, but this was converted to a flat-switched facility in the 1950s.

IC also built one of the largest classification yards in the United States at Markham, on the southern edge of Chicago. The yard opened in 1926 and was then rebuilt as two separate hump yards in 1950, at a cost of $3 million. The northbound classification yard had a 64-track bowl and a very efficient layout, with arrival, classification, and departure roads following each other. This worked well in the 1950s, when train lengths were shorter than today. Now that 8,000-foot manifests are common, however, such a layout would need two or three departure tracks combined to make up a long-distance manifest, blocking the running lines for as much as an hour. The southbound yard at Markham was laid out in a similarly sequential fashion but with a smaller, 48-track classification bowl.

IC, under its general manager, Edward L. Moyers, greatly reduced its yard capacity. In 1989, the southbound hump at Markham was closed, with manifest switching transferred to Glen Yard in Chicago. Just a year later, the northbound hump was closed and its bowl paved over to make IC's main intermodal facility, which was named after Edward Moyers. In 1999, intermodal facilities were expanded at Markham, and much of the southbound bowl was converted to standing room for trailers. The massive IC/CN intermodal and carload yards can be seen clearly when one drives east along I-80. The area surrounding the yard is not a good neighborhood, and it is probably safer to observe while on railroad property than outside the perimeter fence.

Overgrown and largely dismantled, the old hump yard at East St. Louis still was easily recognizable as such during my 1999 visit. The Gateway Arch can be seen through the murky sky on the horizon.

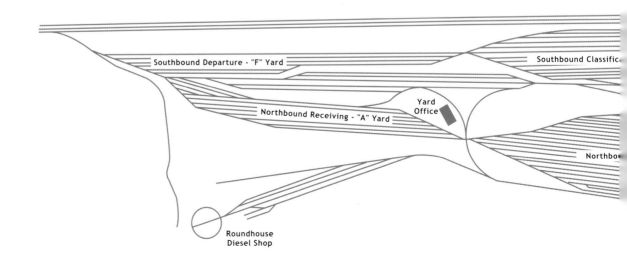

Southbound Departure - "F" Yard

Southbound Classific

Northbound Receiving - "A" Yard

Yard Office

Northbo

Roundhouse
Diesel Shop

Illinois Central had major flat yards in Champaign, Illinois; Jackson, Mississippi; and New Orleans. The latter is seen here. With the city and the Superdome on the horizon, an IC switcher rests at Mays Yard in 1990.

TO CHICAGO ▸

Southbound Receiving - "D" Yard

rd

Repair Facilities

Northbound Departure- "C" Yard

tion - "B" Yard

## MARKHAM YARD

*Drawing by Otto M. Vondrak, 2003.*

# CANADIAN PACIFIC

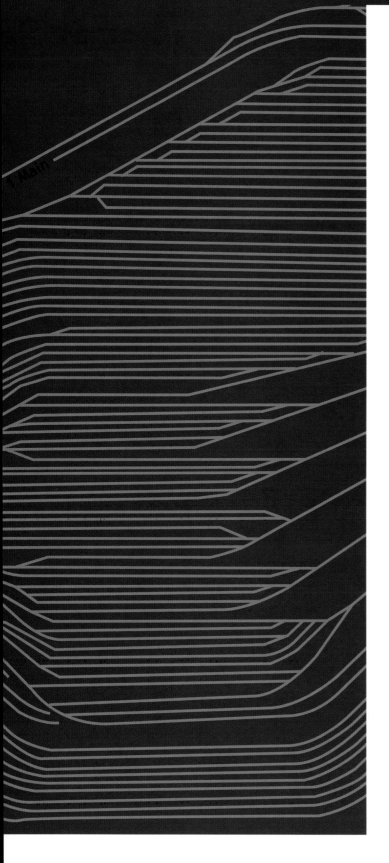

Canadian Pacific (CP), Canada's first transcontinental railroad, was completed in the 1880s. Today, it is CN's smaller sister, with a network of 14,000 miles, extending, like CN, into the northern United States. In the case of CP, two main U.S. railroads give it U.S. links. In the east, the 1,500-mile ex–Delaware & Hudson reaches down as far as Washington. In the Midwest, the Soo Lines covered nearly 5,000 route miles back in 1990, but are somewhat less extensive today. The original CP had four major hump yards in Montreal, Toronto, Winnipeg, and Calgary. All but the yard in Montreal remain operational in 2003. CP also inherited two major hump yards from the Soo Line and its predecessors, at Bensenville in Chicago and at Pig's Eye in St. Paul.

# St. Luc Yard—Montreal, Quebec

St. Luc opened in 1950 at a cost of $13 million. The yard had standing room for 6,524 cars and a 48-track classification bowl. In 1994, the hump closed due to the fall in boxcar traffic and repetitive handling of cars.

Access to the yard is poor. The yard itself lies parallel to the CN facility at Taschereau, on its eastern side. As at Taschereau, there are no convenient overpasses or grade crossings from which to observe the action.

## Yard Departures from St. Luc at Closure in 1994

| TRAIN NUMBER | DEPARTURE | ORIGIN/DESTINATION |
| --- | --- | --- |
| 919 | 00.01 | St. Luc–Toronto |
| 481 | 01.00 | St. Luc–Vancouver |
| 901 | 02.10 | St. Luc–Toronto |
| 471 | 03.25 | St. Luc–Coquitlam |
| 493 | 03.25 | St. Luc–Vancouver |
| 503 | 04.00 | St. Luc–Bensenville |
| 284 | 06.00 | St. Luc–St. John |
| 91 | 07.00 | St. Luc–Lasalle (industry trip) |
| 520 | 07.00 | St. Thérese–Niagara |
| 409 | 07.00 | St. Luc–St. Martin |
| 917 | 07.00 | St. Luc-Thunder Bay |
| 210 | 08.00 | St. Luc–St. Thérese |
| 509 | 08.00 | St. Luc–Detroit Oak Yard |
| 903 | 08.00 | St. Luc–Toronto |
| R83 | 12.15 | St. Luc–Vaudreuil (industry trip) |
| 406 | 13.00 | St. Luc–Trois-Rivières |
| 915 | 17.30 | St. Therese–Windsor (GM traffic) |
| OCR | 18.00 | St. Luc–Adirondack Junction |
| 907 | 19.25 | St. Luc–Toronto |
| 554 | 19.30 | St. Luc–Binghampton |
| 556 | 20.30 | St. Luc–Potomac |
| 929 | 21.30 | Lachine–Toronto |
| 290 | 22.00 | St. Luc–Brownville |
| 491 | 23.00 | St. Luc–Vancouver |
| Newport | 24.00 | St. Luc–Newport |
| 121 | All day | Local transfers (runs three shifts) |

During my visit in 1996, the control tower at St. Luc still stood, supervising a vast expanse of ballast. The switching gear for the classification bowl can be seen here, almost completely intact but covered in months of dust and debris.

The remains of the bowl at St. Luc are seen from the derelict hump tower in October 1996.

# Agincourt Yard—Toronto, Ontario

The CP yard in Toronto is the largest on the network, with 72 classification tracks. It opened in 1966 with 63 tracks, and the final 9 classification tracks were added in 1990, because of increasing carload traffic through Toronto. During a visit in 1996, tower staff said that the previous 24 hours had seen just 982 cars over the hump, which was unusually few. The normal throughput was said to be nearer 1,500 per day. An engine house within the yard is home to more than 170 CP units.

The yard is easy to find in east Toronto. Head east out of the city on Highway 401, then take the McCowan Road Exit northward. The entrance to the yard is on the right, and a bridge over the hump lies just inside the railroad property. To view the other end of the yard, continue north on McCowan and turn right onto Finch Avenue East. This crosses the departure end of the yard on a long overpass, which is a good spot for photography.

This view, taken toward a sunset in October 1996, shows the 72-track classification bowl at Agincourt.

GP9 No. 1558 heads a three-unit lash-up, acting as hump pilot at Agincourt. The engines are pulling back cars that have stopped short of their allocated sidings and need to be re-humped.

A GP9 and a SW1200 team up to pull cars out of the bowl for placement in the departure tracks at Agincourt. This view was taken from the Finch Avenue East overpass.

The Winnipeg yards owned by CP were opened in 1880 and still occupy the same tract of land near the city's center. When they opened, it was boasted that they were some of the most extensive railyards in the world. But how the mighty are fallen! Today there are 18 run-through tracks and two small "mini-hump" yards, for westbound and eastbound cars, respectively. The mini-humps each have 16 reception roads leading to 16 classification tracks and have a much lower profile to the hump. Switching is done at a lower speed than in the bigger yards, with smaller retarders that brake on just one rail, rather than both.

The yards can be observed from several excellent road overpasses, including Arlington Street, McPhillips Street, and Keewatin Street.

The view of Winnipeg Yard, looking east from Keewatin Street, shows the westbound hump with a boxcar about to descend into the bowl. The single rail brakes can also be seen, highlighted by the driving rain on a dreary day in April 1998.

Again looking east from Keewatin Street, a transcontinental run-through manifest draws into one of the 18 long staging tracks. The McPhillips Street overpass can be seen in the background.

Calgary is home to CP headquarters. The yard and locomotive shops there are the major facility of CP's western operations. The engine house at Alyth Yard is responsible for 319 units, more than one-third of the entire CP fleet. The classification yard is a modern, 1960s hump facility, with 18 reception and departure tracks and a 48-track classification bowl. During my visit in 1998, the yard handled between 1,200 and 1,600 cars per 24 hours.

One of the new developments planned for the hump was a global positioning system (GPS), to keep tabs on cars in the terminal area—and also the deer that roamed the classification bowl, no doubt. Because the yard is in a rural location without heavy security, deer are abundant, especially where grain cars spill any of their cargo in the classification bowl—free food for the local wildlife!

The engine house and hump approach tracks can be seen clearly from Blackfoot Trail Avenue in southeast Calgary. The pullout area from the classification bowl can be seen when traveling south on Deerfoot Trail, although it is not possible to stop and take pictures on this highway.

ABOVE: Cars roll over the hump at Alyth Yard. In the background is the large engine house, responsible for more than 300 units.

OPOSTIE PAGE, TOP: With downtown Calgary in the background, a manifest with eight engines up front arrives at Alyth Yard. The picture was taken from the Blackfoot Trail Bridge.

LEFT: This view of Alyth Yard was taken from the pullout tower, at the south end of the classification bowl. A GP9 and a C-424 locomotive pull a string of cars, while a solitary GP9 waits on the right for its next set of instructions.

Old hands at Bensenville in 1995 describe in detail where the arrival tracks used to be and how busy things used to be in "the old days." The switching panel still has all the routes for the 70-track bowl intact, but these routes are no longer used.

This 1995 view shows the last 24 classification tracks at Bensenville. The remains of the rest of the bowl are still evident, especially on the right, where an old retarder stands alone. The exit from it has been concreted over for the new container tracks. One of the approaches to Chicago's O'Hare Airport passes over the bowl. Airline passengers may end up flying right over the yard here.

Through a series of mergers and bankruptcies, CP now owns and operates two ex–Milwaukee Road classification yards. The larger of these is the Chicago hub for CP at Bensenville. The yard has been modernized and upgraded during the late 1990s, to enable it to cope with both carload traffic and ever-increasing block trains and container traffic.

The yard was built in 1953 at a cost of $5.2 million, and it handled more than 3,600 cars per day during the 1950s and 1960s. The 125 miles of track included a 70-track bowl and a fully automated hump, with 16 retarders to slow cars on their descent into the bowl. In 1985, the Soo Line acquired the yard, when it purchased most of the remaining Milwaukee Road infrastructure. The Soo Line has now become part of CP, as a result of which Bensenville's importance as a freight hub has increased considerably.

During my visit in 1995, car classification at Bensenville had fallen to less than 1,000 per day, and the classification bowl had been reduced to just 24 tracks. The old yard had boasted 21 arrival tracks and the large 70-track bowl mentioned above. In 1995, the old hump and retarders were still in place to control the entrance to the central four fans of classification tracks, but plans were well advanced to construct a mini-hump with a lower profile and more modern retarders. Space vacated at the outer edges of the old bowl was rapidly being filled with TOFC tracks, which by 1995 included seven "pig tracks" for TOFC traffic and four container tracks for COFC trains.

Bensenville Yard is just south of Chicago's O'Hare airport. Mannheim Road affords a moderate view of the eastern exit from the yard and also crosses Proviso Yard a couple of miles farther south. The best views of the east end of the yard are glimpsed from I-294, the Illinois (or Tri-State) Tollway, but one cannot stop here. Franklin Road, a left turn off Mannheim Road when traveling north, runs all the way along the southern perimeter of the yard and offers good glimpses of the yard. Finally, at the end of Franklin, a right turn on York Road leads to an overpass at the west end of the yard. The area around the yard seems fairly rough, so caution may be advised.

In 1956, Milwaukee Road opened this yard at a cost of $4.9 million. Its major distinction is that it is the only classification yard able to boast that its entire bowl has been flooded. This happens occasionally when the Mississippi River bursts its banks and floods the nearby Pig's Eye Lake and surroundings.

The yard currently handles just over 1,000 cars every day and, from a railfan's point of view, is one of the best spots for watching freight trains. The yard is in pleasant surroundings, with excellent access from public places. It also has the BNSF and UP mainlines running by, which boosts traffic passing the yard by a factor of three or more.

The yard has five arrival tracks that lead to a fully automated hump, which recently had its control systems updated. The classification bowl has 34 tracks, numbered 6 through 41, which serve five departure tracks.

Finding the best spots to observe the action at Pig's Eye can be a challenge, even with a detailed map. The best way to is to leave I-494 north at the exit for Highway 61. Traveling north on 61, you can see the yard on the left, but you cannot readily turn left to get to it. Continue north until well past the yard. Turn left at the traffic light at Warner Road, and continue down Warner, branching left over the northern approaches to Pig's Eye. This provides several excellent spots to observe the yard and also the adjacent UP yard and passing BNSF traffic.

Then, travel back up Warner Road and, at the traffic light where it intersects Highway 61, turn right, heading south. After a couple of miles, you can park at a lot for CP staff, which also has a convenient footbridge over the mainlines to the yard tower. The views from here are excellent.

No matter how automated a hump yard, you still need a car cutter to separate the cars in the appropriate places for classification. The cutter is oblivious to the large telephoto lens bearing down on him.

Dappled sunlight catches the cars of this manifest as it is propelled from one of five receiving tracks at Pig's Eye. The modern digital display at the hump is identical to that installed by UP at the new Davis Yard.

A CP yardmaster explains the workings of the hump at Pig's Eye on a Sunday afternoon. Cars roll down into the classification bowl on a day when well over 1,000 cars were classified.

A northbound unit of grain-car empties passes Pig's Eye in an unseasonably cold October 2002. On the left is the BNSF autorack yard, with the exit from Pig's Eye in the middle distance. To the right are the shops at Pig's Eye, and farther right, out of picture, lies the UP yard. This spot is one of the busiest and best in the United States for watching a wide variety of freight trains in action.

LEFT: This view from the footbridge off Highway 61 shows a BNSF TOFC heading south, with St. Paul and then the Pig's Eye bowl in the background. Views to the north and south here are excellent.

This directory of North American classification yards was written between 1989 and 2002, and for much of this time, Conrail was a thriving northeastern railroad, responsible for nearly a dozen major classification yards. After CSX's and NS's 1998 takeover, however, Conrail's yards were reallocated to these two remaining big eastern railroads. Most of the research and photography for this book were undertaken when the yards and terminals were under Conrail ownership, so this section of the book is allocated to the late, great Conrail.

Conrail began in April 1976 as the final resolution for the railroads of the northeastern United States. Six major railroads had gone bankrupt, one by one, in the preceding five years. They formed the new Conrail, which received a several-billion-dollar subsidy from the U.S. Treasury. Penn Central (a merger of the New York Central and Pennsylvania Railroads) was the largest of the merger partners and was joined by the Reading, Lehigh Valley, Lehigh & Hudson, Erie Lackawanna, and the Central Railroad of New Jersey.

In 2003, 10 hump yards survive from the Conrail era, as well as many other yards that used to be much larger but now find themselves bypassed or redundant, due to streamlining of carload traffic. Among the latter category are three of the largest yards ever built in the United States—Altoona, Enola, and Syracuse, discussed at the end of the chapter. The remnants of these three yards can still be clearly seen, although the days when they each handled more than 10,000 cars per day are long gone.

The northeastern United States is littered with patches of wasteland that were once mighty freight yards. One of the largest is at Cedar Hill, New Hampshire, once a major Penn Central yard with two separate hump complexes. In 1999, this Providence & Worcester freight is seen in the midst of the old complex, on land once occupied by the northbound classification bowl. The yard still has a few tracks and is used by CSX as well as the Providence & Worcester.

The New York Central Railroad opened the Big Four Yard in Indianapolis (also called Avon Yard) in 1960, at a cost of $14 million. With the merger with the Pennsylvania Railroad, it acquired work from Hawthorne Yard in downtown Indianapolis. The yard is said to have had the ideal pullout arrangements for the classification bowl: two parallel tracks allowed simultaneous pullout of cars from the bowl, and two long spurs at the east end of the yard allowed pullout without interfering with the mainlines passing the yard.

During my visit in 1995, the yardmaster, Rex Simmons, explained that just over 1,500 cars had been classified in the previous 24 hours. The receiving yard could hold 10 trains, from where cars were drawn back onto two hump leads. The hump itself fed six fans with a total of 55 tracks and 12 long departure tracks.

The yard is out in the country, west of Indianapolis, and does not offer many easy viewpoints from public places. To find the yard, travel west from Indianapolis on U.S. Highway 36. Turn left onto an overpass over the hump lead called Dan Jones Road, from which pictures may be taken.

Rex Simmons sits astride his control panel in 1995, as cars are classified at Avon Yard.

On the right, an Avon-to-Conway manifest leaves the east end of the complex at Avon. On the left, another engine busies itself on pullout duty. As can be seen, this takes place on a separate spur from the tracks needed for arrivals and departures.

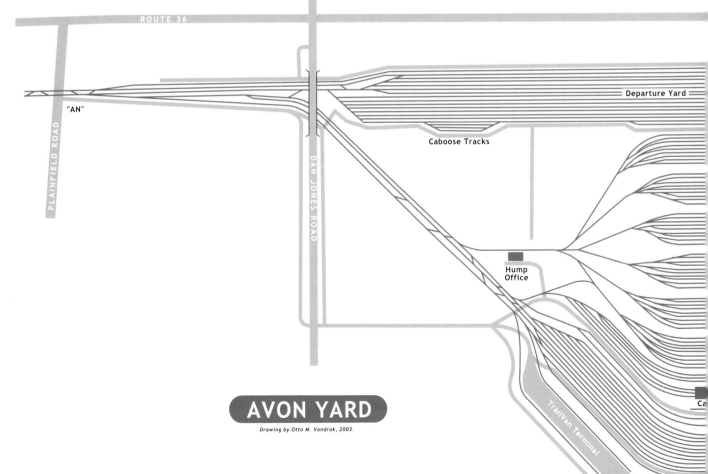

ROUTE 36

PLAINFIELD ROAD

"AN"

DAN JONES ROAD

Departure Yard

Caboose Tracks

Hump Office

TrailVan Terminal

Ca

## AVON YARD

*Drawing by Otto M. Vondrak, 2003.*

Sunrise over the hump at Avon Yard, and a pair of covered coil cars descend the hump into the rising mist. This picture was printed by Gene Nocon, of San Diego, who is well known for his black-and-white photographic print work.

SHELTON DR.

ROUTE 36

1050 E.

"MY"

Caboose Tracks

Diesel
Shop

eceiving Yard

Conrail reports in a brochure that Elkhart Yard, just more than 100 miles east of Chicago in rural Indiana, is the busiest in the system. Unfortunately, as is often the case, railroad literature cannot be believed. Conway Yard, near Pittsburgh, is far busier. That said, the ex-New York Central (NYC) yard in Elkhart is by far the second busiest on Conrail.

The yard, which NYC opened in 1956 at a cost of $14 million, is distinctive for having the largest classification bowl of any hump yard in the United States (only the CN yards at Toronto and Montreal are as large or larger). When opened, the yard covered 675 acres and consisted of 15 receiving tracks, a 72-track bowl, and 14 departure tracks. It handled 74 trains daily, not all of which were classified over the hump, with a capacity to handle 2,800 cars daily over the single hump.

Between 1979 and 1982, Conrail invested substantially in the facility and expanded its capacity to 3,200 cars per day. This was done by first lengthening 14 of the tracks in the classification bowl to hold 50 cars instead of just 25. Also, one track was added to the receiving yard and two to the departure yard, and two pullout tracks were built to more efficiently remove cars from the classification bowl.

During my visit in 1995, 850 cars were humped each shift, or 2,550 per day. By the time of my second visit in 2002, throughput was down, but the yard still handled more than 2,000 cars per day over the hump.

The arrivals during the 24 hours prior to my visit in May 1995 were from the following destinations, listed in order:

Cicero
Avon
Selkirk
Conway
U.S. Steel (Pittsburgh)
Proviso
Frontier
Grand Rapids
Clearing
Lansing
Columbus
Streeter, Illinois (Santa Fe)
Proviso
Cicero
Blue Island
Bethlehem Steel
Avon
Kankakee, Illinois (Santa Fe)
Stirling Yard (Detroit)
Chicago Junction
EJ&E Illinois
Fort Wayne
Toledo
Columbus
Conway
Wayne Yard (Detroit)
Santa Fe exchange
Avon

This view from the tower at Elkhart shows cars being drawn out of the receiving yard for transfer directly to the departure yard, avoiding the hump. This was an unusual maneuver but greatly reduced the transit time of these cars. The West Indiana Avenue overpass can be seen in the distance.

During my visit to Elkhart in 2002, the yardmaster immediately recognized me as the "mad English surgeon" who had visited the yard seven years earlier, in 1995. He was kind enough let me spend a few freezing minutes trying to capture this view of the hump in operation.

This totals 28 arrivals from a wide range of locations! Not only all major Conrail yards, but also GTW locations in Michigan and several major interchange yards in Chicago and Illinois are listed here, making Elkhart a real Midwest melting pot. All the tracks at Elkhart can accommodate 6,197 60-foot cars, or nearly 10,000 of the previous standard-sized 40-foot boxcars.

The yard at Elkhart is a huge complex, but is not easily seen while driving down Elkhart's main street. The yard lies on the southwestern outskirts of the town and is largely hidden from public view behind trees. Drive west on West Franklin Street (old U.S. Highway 933) and turn left onto North Nappanee Street, heading south, which becomes South Nappanee Street. After one passes under the east end of the yard, access is possible via a right turn from South Nappanee Street onto Markle Street, then right on Florence Avenue. There is no easy public access to the yard. One other spot to observe arrivals is from the overpass on West Indiana Avenue, which crosses the eastern end of the reception yard.

The sheer size of the bowl at Elkhart can be appreciated in this view, looking west from the hump tower in 1995.

RIGHT: The daily manifest from Stirling Yard in Detroit is propelled over the Elkhart hump. The train is made up of cars carrying mainly auto parts or steel. The receiving yard is seen in the background; the tinted windows of the hump tower are on the right.

Allentown has had a yard since the turn of the century. The facility was owned by the Central Railroad of New Jersey and was a major interchange point for traffic to and from the Reading Railroad. Two small hump yards, a westbound and an eastbound, were crammed into the flood plain on the northern edge of the Lehigh River.

In 1972, the Central of New Jersey ceased operations, and the Lehigh Valley Railroad took over Allentown Yard. This takeover was short-lived, and the yard became part of Conrail in 1976. It still had two antiquated manual humps and was not designed for the typical 100-car manifest of the 1970s. Modernization was badly needed.

In 1978, the yard was completely rebuilt, with a single hump facing westbound. The yard became more important under Conrail, as traffic patterns were revised to try to keep as much freight traffic as possible away from the busy Northeast Corridor. The new yard has 6 reception tracks that lead to 29 classification tracks. The hump has one primary retarder and four secondary or group retarders, which are all fully automated. Cars ready to depart are pulled out from the classification bowl in the usual fashion, but the yard has no dedicated departure yard. Therefore, when two or more classification tracks need their cars combined, the exit to the yard may be blocked for up to an hour.

During my visit in 1996, the hump handled just 250 cars per shift, or four trains. This was down considerably when compared to the activity in the early 1980s, when it handled 1,200 cars per day. The main destinations for manifest traffic were Oak Island in New York, Conway and Buffalo to the west, and Hagerstown to the south, for exchange with Norfolk Southern. Freight trips also ran from the yard to Bethlehem and Philadelphia.

Although it was completely rebuilt in the late 1970s, the yard has an old-world feel about it. Surrounded by public access points and set in a pleasant rural locale, it is also one of the most enjoyable in the United States to

Two high-powered units arrive at the hump in Allentown in March 1996. This manifest is from Oak Island Yard in New Jersey and will be reclassified here. The road between Allentown and Bethlehem can be seen in the foreground, along with the author's rental car. The railroad really is in excellent proximity to the public road here.

With the public road on the right, this view shows the Allentown hump in action. As can be seen, the yard is squeezed onto the north bank of the Lehigh River.

observe and photograph. It lies south of downtown Allentown, on the north bank of the Lehigh River. A paved road along the northern perimeter of the yard links Allentown to Bethlehem and affords excellent views of the hump area and reception sidings. At the other end of the yard, to the west, all departures from the complex can be observed from the park in Allentown, which is even blessed with picnic facilities—railfan heaven!

Conrail No. 8131 looks for all the world as if it is simply shunting a couple of cars. This view at the west end of Allentown Yard is in fact a picture of the Allentown–West Philadelphia manifest, which has only two cars for exchange with CSX on this Saturday in March 1996.

Departures from the west end of the yard could block the mainline for over an hour. This was the case with the daily ALHA (Allentown–Hagerstown) manifest, seen here awaiting departure from the yard.

ABOVE: This view from the footbridge to the Allentown hump tower shows the classification bowl well, as a manifest from Oak Island to the yard is placed into the bowl for safety over the weekend.

RIGHT: Two miles east of Allentown Yard, the tracks cross the Lehigh River to rejoin the old Lehigh Valley bypass route to the yard. Here, an Allentown-Oak Island manifest heads east in March 1996, with more than 100 cars in tow.

This is by far the largest yard on the old Conrail system and was for many years the largest and busiest in the United States. Only the recent explosion in traffic through North Platte has relegated this aging behemoth to second place. As late as 1983, a sign outside the yard proclaimed it "the largest push-button yard in the U.S.A."

Conway is located 22 miles northwest of downtown Pittsburgh and is the only dual hump yard on ex-Conrail territory. The yard we see today is the result of a rebuild in 1956 by Penn Central, which provided a pair of hump classification yards on the northern bank of the Ohio River.

In the early twentieth century, Conway was one of four large yards that the Pennsylvania Railroad built. These yards each had the capacity to hold approximately 10,000 cars and often classified that many every 24 hours. They were situated at Enola (10,705 cars), Altoona (10,500 cars), Harrisburg (10,015 cars), and Conway (8,967 cars). By the 1920s, the capacity at Altoona had been expanded to 14,000 cars and the yard at Harrisburg had been downgraded, leaving the big three yards of the Pennsylvania system at Enola, Altoona, and Conway.

Jumping forward to the twenty-first century, only Conway continues to flourish. The yard still dispatches 90,000 to 100,000 cars every month, but this is only 60 percent of its potential capacity to classify 6,000 cars daily. The yard covers 568 acres on the east bank of the Ohio River and contains two completely separate hump systems.

The eastbound yard (which actually runs from north to south) has 10 receiving tracks, a 54-track classification bowl, and 10 dispatching tracks. The westbound yard (running from south to north) is almost a mirror image, with 11 receiving tracks, a 53-track classification bowl, and 10 dispatching tracks. The eastbound yard is semiautomatic, with the controller having input into the control of the rail brakes in the classification bowl, whereas the westbound yard is fully automated. The improvements of the 1956 rebuild mean that the Conway of today has the capacity to hold more than 11,000 cars on 181 miles of track, which makes it the second largest yard in the United States.

The yard at Conway is not easy to see clearly, although a left turn off Route 65 leads to a small bridge over the southern exit from the yard. The next side road is north of the yard, and views of the yard in action can really only be seen from railroad land.

A manifest from Conway to Oak Island in New Jersey winds south out of Conway Yard in 1998. Behind the head-end power on the right of the picture is a Conrail switcher, which will propel cars along the westbound receiving tracks to the westbound hump. This view was taken from the small side road off Route 65, south of the yard.

This view was taken from the main yard tower at Conway. Stretching away to the north is the westbound classification bowl, while on the left are the receiving tracks for the eastbound classification yard. Toward the base of the window view are both Norfolk Sothern and Conrail engines waiting to return to the servicing facilities at Conway, where they will be refueled and maybe also have a 1,000-mile inspection.

Selkirk Yard was opened in 1924 as part of a larger scheme to bypass the congested rail facilities in Albany, called the Castleton cutoff. New York Central had a large yard at West Albany, and during the early 1920s, more than 8,000 cars passed through it every day. Not only were the facilities stretched to breaking point by this amount of traffic, but the gradient on the eastern approaches to West Albany necessitated pusher locomotives. This made the passage of freight trains through this bottleneck very labor intensive and, therefore, expensive.

The Selkirk Yard of the 1920s was two separate hump yards, one for eastbound traffic and one for westbound. The 700-acre site had the potential for a yard with 250 miles of track and capacity for 20,000 cars. In the end, a smaller set of yards was built, with room for 11,000 cars. The new yards at Selkirk were some of the first to use "floodlighting," with electricity purchased from the local power utility.

In 1966, New York Central started a complete rebuild of the Selkirk yards, converting the two separate hump facilities into a single large "push-button" hump yard. The yard was completed in 1968 and named after Alfred E. Perlman, CEO of New York Central Railroad. The final cost of the rebuild was $29 million.

The yard is like the one Norfolk Southern built at Bellevue, Ohio, or like a yard farther afield, such as Munchen Nord in Munich, Germany. It has space for extra classification tracks. The original plans had room for 90 classification tracks, but only 70 were installed. The spare

This view of Selkirk Yard, looking south from the Old School Road Bridge, shows a Conrail lash-up arriving with a manifest from the south. The train winds under the hump, where another manifest is being classified, and will draw forward to the receiving yard, which is behind where this photograph was taken.

land on either side of the 70-track bowl has never been needed. Had these tracks been built, Selkirk would have overtaken Taschereau as the largest classification bowl in the world.

The yard of today is busy, with a throughput of 2,500 cars every day and the capacity to classify as many as 3,200. Eleven receiving tracks can hold 1,716 cars. The 70 tracks in the classification bowl can hold 3,680 cars. The longest of these is 70 cars long, and the shortest has 37 cars. The yard has nine north departure tracks and five south departure tracks, as well as four run-through roads. The longest of the departure tracks can hold an amazing 280 cars. Including the local yard and other sidings, total yard capacity is 8,500 cars.

Selkirk is perhaps one of the easiest and most enjoyable yards in North America to observe and photograph. It lies in a rural setting 9 miles southwest of Albany. Several road bridges cross the facility, including a 400-yard-long bridge over the engine house and hump area.

To reach the yard, leave Albany on Delaware Avenue (Route 443). Turn left on Elm Avenue (Route 32). After 3 miles, this road crosses the entrance to the receiving yard as well as the departure tracks for northbound traffic. Just before the bridge, take the left turn at Crebble Road and continue for just over a mile. Turn right onto Old School Road (Route 53), which brings you onto the long bridge over the engine house and hump area. After crossing this bridge, turn left and follow South Albany Road to a T-junction with Bridge Street. Turn left here, which will bring you to a bridge over the pullout end of the classification bowl.

By 1999, when this picture was taken from the pullout tower to the south of the bowl at Selkirk, CSX owned and operated the yard. The three-way motive power split on this COFC run-through train reflects Conrail's recent history.

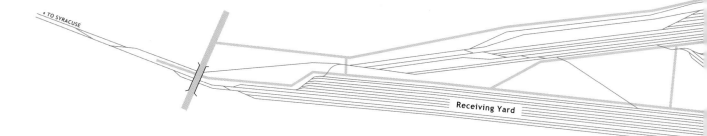

◄ TO SYRACUSE

Receiving Yard

**SELKIRK YARD**

*Drawing by Otto M. Vondrak, 2003.*

Motive power from all the major American railroads can be seen at Selkirk, as this view from the Old School Road overpass illustrates.

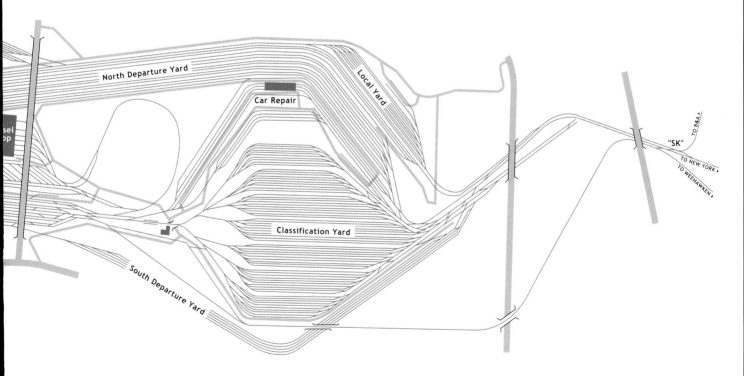

North Departure Yard

Local Yard

Car Repair

sel
op

Classification Yard

South Departure Yard

"SK"

TO B&A ▶

TO NEW YORK ▶

TO WEEHAWKEN ▶

This view of the receiving yard was taken from the Old School Road overpass. In the distance is the bridge on Elm Avenue. Manifest traffic for classification is on the right. The train of autoracks and the short container train are both run-through services.

Selkirk is the funnel through which virtually all traffic from the East Coast between New York and Maine must pass. This view, taken in 1996, shows a typical double-stack train waiting for a crew change at Selkirk. The trailing load numbered 200 stack cars.

Looking south from Elm Avenue in 1996: a mixed trio of C&NW, UP, and Conrail power leaves Selkirk's north departure yard with a manifest for the west. To the right are the tracks of the receiving yard.

Traffic from Montreal arrives at Selkirk via former Delaware & Hudson trackage two or three times a day. This container train has an aging Alco as the second engine in its head-end power. The cars to the left of the CP train are being propelled to the hump, which can be seen to the left of the light blue yard tower in the background.

# Frontier Yard—Buffalo, New York

Frontier Yard was the first electronically controlled hump yard built by the New York Central Railroad. It opened in 1957 at a cost of $10.5 million and remains the major classification facility in Buffalo today. For the majority of its existence, it has been owned by Conrail, but it now belongs to CSX. The yard has a 63-track classification bowl and a total of 120 tracks, including a local yard and receiving and departure roads. Shoehorned into a residential area of Buffalo, the yard is surprisingly busy. During my visit in 1996, it was classifying between 2,200 and 3,000 cars every day over the hump.

The CSX (ex-Conrail) mainline as well as the arrival yard and hump approach can be viewed from Harlem Road in Buffalo. The departure end of the yard is not visible from a public place.

Viewed from the hump tower at Frontier in 1996, the cars of an SYBU manifest roll down the hump. The train had arrived a couple of hours earlier from DeWitt Yard in Syracuse, New York, bringing 106 cars to be classified at Frontier Yard.

This view of the arrival tracks at Frontier Yard emphasizes the cramped nature of the site. The arrival tracks are packed with manifests from local industries and cross-border traffic from Canada. Wrapping the arrival and departure tracks around the classification bowl has greatly reduced the length needed for the site, although at the expense of operational efficiency.

Frontier's 63-track classification bowl is seen from the hump tower. The second hump building is for controlling the retarders.

A Conrail yard goat (with attached slave unit) propels cars over the hump at Frontier. This view was taken from Harlem Road.

# Stanley Yard—Toledo, Ohio

The Toledo & Ohio Central Railroad opened Stanley Yard in 1913. It was rebuilt as a hump yard as long ago as 1930, although automated retarders were added much later. By 1996, under Conrail, the yard was quite run down and classified only 450 to 700 cars per day. The six arrival tracks and 42-track classification bowl are now somewhat busier under CSX ownership, and the threat of closure to the hump seems to have receded, especially as CSX ripped up its own hump yard at Walbridge in 1993.

The yard stands in open country to the south of town, across the Maumee River. Route 795 crosses the southern approach to the hump. Exit onto East Broadway from 795 and head north, which allows you to drive along the yard's eastern border. Turn left at the crossroads with Walbridge Road. There is a lengthy flat crossing over the pullout area of the yard.

In April 1997, Conrail 6996 shunts the departure end of the bowl at Stanley Yard. The engines on the left, headed by 6998, will make up the head-end power for TOPI, the daily manifest to Pittsburgh's Conway Yard. In the background, several manifests are lined up in the departure roads.

The daily GTW manifest from Detroit arrives at Stanley. The train is made up almost exclusively of traffic related to the automotive industry.

Stanley's 42-track classification bowl, viewed from the hump crest in 1997. At this time, the hump was operational only for one shift per day. Since the CSX takeover, things have become busier.

Buckeye opened in 1970 by Penn Central, is the most recently constructed of the ex-Conrail hump yards. The total cost of the yard was $26 million, $1.8 million of which was spent on road overpasses, of which five were built. Two of these provide excellent spots for photography.

The yard is a modern push-button facility, with hump shunting and classification operating in a fully automated fashion. It covers 453 acres and has room for 4,510 cars. As seen in other yards mentioned in this book, the original plans envisaged some expansion at a later date, with room for extra arrival, classification, and departure tracks. However, none of these have been built yet.

Originally there was room for 60 classification tracks, but only 40 have been built. Similarly, there was room for 9 receiving and 10 departure tracks, but the yard has only 7

and 8 of these, respectively. The design capacity of the yard was 2,400 cars per 24 hours, but during my visit in 1997, it classified only 1,800 cars per day.

The Penn Central article publicizing the opening of Buckeye reveals the orderly nature of the classification bowl. Each track had a permanent allocation, such that track No. 14 received traffic for Buffalo Frontier Yard and track No. 27 for Enola. Eight of the tracks were allocated to other major yards on Conrail, while another seven were for traffic to other railroads and the rest for local destinations.

The yard lies approximately 5 miles west of downtown Columbus and is easy to watch and photograph. From the north, there is an excellent view over the hump from Roberts Road. From the south, the pullout operation from the classification can be seen well from Trabue Road.

On a very dull day in April 1997, Conrail engines line up at the southern end of the classification bowl at Buckeye Yard. The pullout operation here has been cited as one of the most efficient on Conrail because two parallel tracks serve each half of the classification bowl. This allows pullout to take place at twice the speed that it does in some less well-designed yards.

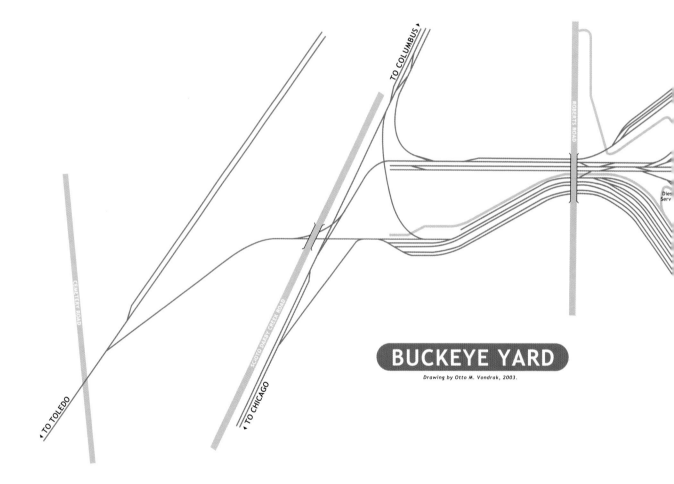

BUCKEYE YARD

*Drawing by Otto M. Vondrak, 2003.*

TO COLUMBUS ►

ROBERTS ROAD

Dies
Serv

CEMETERY ROAD

SCIOTO DARBY CREEK ROAD

◄ TO TOLEDO

◄ TO CHICAGO

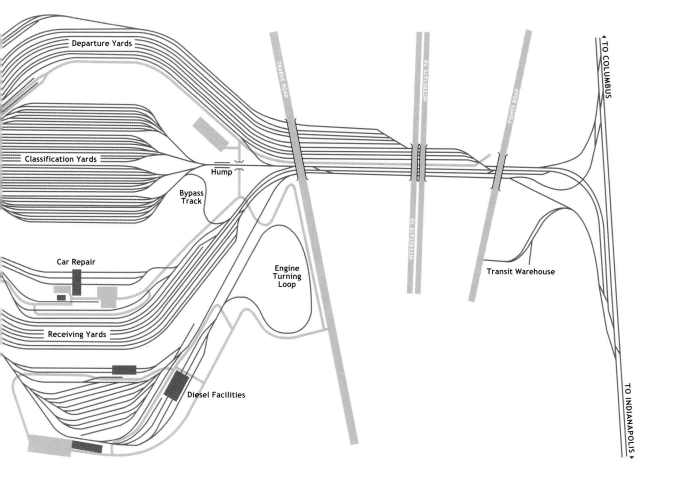

Departure Yards

Classification Yards

Hump

Bypass Track

Car Repair

Receiving Yards

Engine Turning Loop

Diesel Facilities

TRABUE ROAD

INTERSTATE 70

INTERSTATE 70

FISHER ROAD

Transit Warehouse

◄ TO COLUMBUS

TO INDIANAPOLIS ▶

The view of Buckeye from Roberts Road shows the 22-foot-high hump crest, where a Conrail yard slug and slave unit rest after having completed the hump shunting of a recent arrival.

The parallel pullout tracks from the bowl at Columbus are seen clearly in this view from Traube Road, taken in 1997.

These two East Coast yards are unusual, in that ownership remains shared by CSX and Norfolk Southern. Both are small facilities, located in the midst of urban congestion.

Oak Island Yard was built by the Lehigh Valley Railroad; the hump was opened around 1903. Railroad officials from the North Eastern Railway in England visited this yard around 1904 and were given a demonstration of "summit switching." During this demonstration, the yard dealt with two trains, a total of 153 cars and 96 "cuts," in 42 minutes. A 1906 article in *Railroad Gazette* goes to great lengths to point out that this included the time it took the hump engine to return to the arrival tracks and attach to the second train. The actual time the cars from the two trains took to be propelled over the hump was 13 hours and 11 minutes, respectively. Further data reveal that 253,551 cars were run over the eastbound hump at Oak Island for more than 12 months, with only $800 of damage due to the summit switching.

The Oak Island Yard of today is the only major yard in the metropolitan New York area. The 10 arrival tracks lead to an automated hump and 30 classification tracks, which are quite short. Nine departure roads are laid out along the northern border of the classification bowl. During my visit in 1999, the yard classified 800 to 1,000 cars per day. The complex can be viewed from Doremus Avenue, which crosses the departure end of the bowl. An approach road does cross the hump area, but stopping along here is not allowed.

Pavonia is in Camden, New Jersey, 3 miles east of downtown Philadelphia. It has a 32-track classification bowl, with 15 arrival and departure roads placed alongside the bowl. There are road overpasses at both the north and south ends of the classification bowl.

The bowl at Oak Island is seen from the hump crest. The modernized Conrail tower is clearly seen on the right of the picture. The road bridge in the distance is Doremus Avenue.

This view, taken on a dull day in March 1996, shows the westbound hump at Enola. All the towers and retarders are still in position, although the last cars had rolled this way nearly three years earlier. In 2002 though, these tracks were reopened.

Enola Yard was constructed to relieve pressure on the nearby Harrisburg freight yards, across the Susquehanna River. In Harrisburg at the turn of the century, an expanse of tracks totaling 109 miles of sidings had room for more than 10,000 cars. The tracks were always congested, and the Pennsylvania Railroad therefore built the yard at Enola in 1906.

The original layout of the yard when opened was of separate westbound and eastbound complexes. The westbound side had 20 receiving tracks, each with a capacity of 90 cars, and a classification yard with 25 tracks, each with a capacity of 110 cars. Such long classification tracks relieved the need for a separate departure yard, as whole manifests could be assembled in one classification track.

The eastbound yards comprised a receiving yard of 21 tracks, with room for 90 cars each, and a classification bowl of 17 tracks, with room for 70 cars each. A fast-freight yard for through traffic that did not need reclassifying had six tracks, each 70 cars long. The whole site had room for 10,705 cars.

Enola became the major yard at the eastern end of the Pennsylvania Railroad and continued to expand. It had a major rebuild in 1938, when automatic retarders replaced the riders on the eastbound hump. In 1944, the westbound hump was similarly modernized, cutting the time to classify cars by 20 percent. The layout also changed significantly, with westbound classification done through 16 receiving tracks and an enlarged bowl of 35 tracks. Eastbound work was then undertaken through 15 receiving tracks and a 33-track bowl.

The volume of traffic also grew as the yard took over almost completely from the yards in Harrisburg. In 1906, the yard was said to handle 7,000 cars each day, of which as many as 5,000 were classified over its two humps. By 1939, the yard handled an average of 11,207 cars daily, and by October 1941, the daily average reached 14,100. The one-day record for traffic at Enola was set in June 1943, when 20,660 cars passed through the yard on a single day.

After World War II, Enola remained the major yard on the Pennsy and was further improved to allow longer trains to use the facility. Tracks were lengthened to permit manifests of up to 144 cars. In 1953, the yard handled 11,000 cars per day, and its engine house was home to 248 diesels, 90 electrics, and 90 steam engines. From 1940 to 1950, Enola held the honor of being the largest freight yard in the world, but in 1956, it lost the crown to the completely rebuilt Conway Yard.

With the arrival of Conrail in 1976, freight traffic was diverted from Enola because most eastbound freights used the Reading Railroad and Lehigh Valley lines. This led to their being directed over the Rockville Bridge and through Harrisburg, on the other side of the Susquehanna River. It was also decided to abandon the electric network so carefully constructed by the Pennsylvania Railroad, and Enola was de-electrified in 1983. At the same time, Conrail closed the eastbound hump. The closure of direct access from Enola to New York in 1988 left the yard as a stub-end facility. On October 3, 1993, the westbound hump finally closed, ending 87 years of continuous classification at Enola.

This, however, is not the end of the story. Conrail and its predecessors concentrated on east-west traffic. The yard at Allentown had been more than capable of coping with this work since the 1993 closure of Enola. When Conrail was split between CSX and NS in 1999, NS became the new owner of the tracks at Enola. The new railroad, thus created, had an equal emphasis on north-south manifest traffic, and Allentown was not appropriately positioned for this.

NS spent $1.9 million to rebuild some tracks in the old westbound bowl, for a flat classification yard. This increased daily capacity from 125 cars to more than 600, with capacity for more should the need arise. Enola switches north-south traffic formerly handled in the Allentown and Conway yards. In January 2002, NS introduced new manifest schedules, with four new trains using a born-again Enola Yard. The four new services allowed NS to cancel 11 other manifest trains. A small rebirth at Enola, perhaps, but the site of what was once the world's largest classification yard is back in action again.

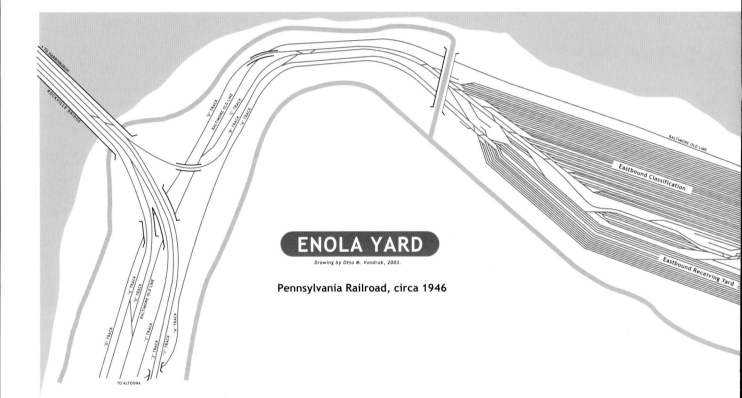

ENOLA YARD

Drawing by Otto M. Vondrak, 2003.

Pennsylvania Railroad, circa 1946

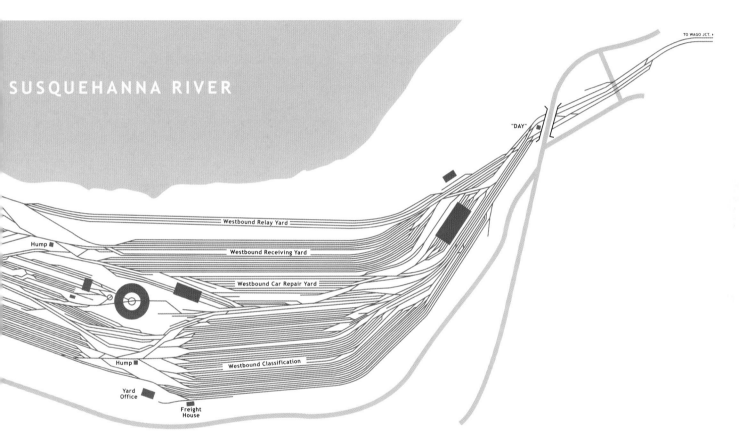

SUSQUEHANNA RIVER

TO WAGO JCT. ▸

"DAY"

Westbound Relay Yard

Hump ▪

Westbound Receiving Yard

Westbound Car Repair Yard

Hump ▪

Westbound Classification

Yard
Office

Freight
House

# Altoona Yard—Altoona, Pennsylvania

Altoona never benefited from a completely automated hump yard, but it was one of the largest yards in the United States at the turn of the century. The Pennsylvania Railroad also modernized it during the 1940s and added retarders to the humps. Today it may still be seen, even though much of the land it formerly occupied is replaced by mature vegetation. The classification tracks that remain in the eastbound bowl are used to store old, surplus Conrail cars.

In the early 1900s, the yard handled 70 trains per day and had trackwork with the capacity to hold 10,500 cars. Only a small portion of this was taken up by a hump yard, which had riders that fed a 15-track classification bowl. The rebuilding during the 1940s provided two semi-automated humps. The yard was crucial in splitting trains due to the climb around Horseshoe Curve in the Allegheny Mountains. With the introduction of high-powered diesels, trains no longer needed to be split for the journey west. In addition, local coal production has fallen and is increasingly handled by block trains, which no longer need marshaling. With faster and longer trains, the yards at Allentown and Conway are more than enough to classify most east-west traffic.

The eastbound classification yard is still very much intact at Altoona. There is a lengthy road bridge across the old yard at Altoona, and the extensive remains of the yards can be easily viewed. The storage of old freight cars in the classification bowl is seen clearly.

The line past Altoona is still a busy freight artery, but coal now travels in unit trains, as seen here in 1999. Behind the unit train, which has paused alongside the yard for a crew change, are a few tracks for local carload traffic.

The largest yard the New York Central Railroad ever built was DeWitt, in Syracuse. DeWitt Yard was unique in that it was the first yard in the United States to have a completely logical layout—that is to say, where receiving tracks flowed onto classification and then departure tracks. Because of the space constraints, either receiving or departure tracks were often placed parallel to the classification bowl in many hump yards, necessitating a pullback of cars prior to humping or makeup of departures.

The layout in 1906 consisted of two separate hump systems. Eastbound had 10 receiving tracks, a 37-track classification bowl, and 16 departure roads. This compared to the westbound system, which had nine receiving tracks, a 30-track bowl, and 23 departure lines. The yard also had several other sections, including sidings for local classification and storage. All told, the tracks had room for more than 10,000 cars. At the time, the yard classified 5,000 cars each day, 2,500 in each direction.

Today, the site of the old DeWitt yards is still a great place to watch trains. The yard is east of downtown Syracuse and is best seen from Seeley Road, which crosses the whole site on a lengthy bridge.

The remains of the eastbound hump are clearly seen behind this manifest arriving at DeWitt Yard from Frontier Yard. The 126 cars will be flat-switched in the remains of the eastbound classification bowl, which can still be switched from the eastern end. The old eastbound receiving yard has been converted into a small intermodal yard, seen behind the train.

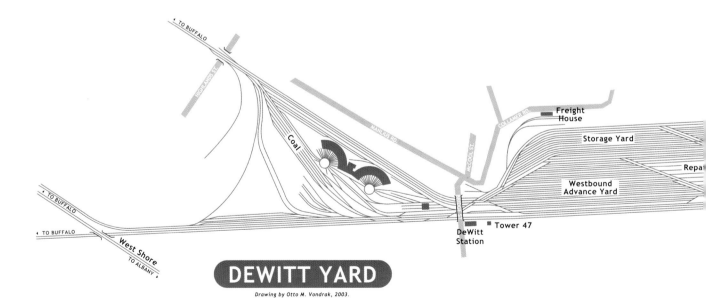

DEWITT YARD

*Drawing by Otto M. Vondrak, 2003.*

The tower and lighting masts give some clue as to the former importance of DeWitt Yard, which was a major junction for lines to Montreal and New York. This picture, taken in 1999, shows the remains of the eastbound classification bowl.

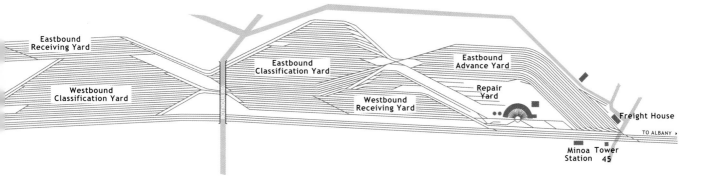

Eastbound
Receiving Yard

Westbound
Classification Yard

Eastbound
Classification Yard

Westbound
Receiving Yard

Eastbound
Advance Yard

Repair
Yard

Freight House

TO ALBANY ▸

Minoa  Tower
Station  45

CSX was formed in 1980 when the Seaboard Coast Line merged with the Chessie System. The network had 11 major hump yards, 9 of which still hump cars today. Since the Conrail carve-up of 1999, CSX also inherited the yards at Indianapolis, Buffalo, Selkirk, and Toledo (Stanley).

The origins of the CSX yards from 1980 include the Louisville & Nashville (L&N), which had already built large classification yards in Birmingham, Nashville, Atlanta, and DeCoursey (near Cincinnati). The last of these four closed in the early 1980s, as the new Queensgate Yard in Cincinnati went into full operation.

The Baltimore & Ohio (B&O) had yards at Cumberland and Willard, Maryland, while the Chesapeake & Ohio (C&O) had its main hump yards in Russell, Kentucky, and in Toledo (Walbridge). Farther south, the Seaboard systems had three big yards in Louisville, Kentucky; Hamlet, North Carolina; and Waycross, Georgia. From this diverse heritage comes the CSX tally of 13 automated hump classification yards, second only to its eastern competitor, Norfolk Southern, which still has 14 operational hump yards in 2003.

This view was taken from a Western Hills viaduct in 1995. Looking north, the yard tower at Queensgate dominates the view as a yard slug with an auxiliary power unit near the hump summit. To the right of the tower, a CSX manifest arrives from the north and will pass on one of the arrival tracks, some of which are 200 cars long.

Queensgate Yard is one of the largest single-capacity projects in contemporary American railroad history. The Chessie System began building this modern, 6,000-car-capacity yard along the valley floor to the west of downtown Cincinnati while continuing to operate the smaller yards eventually built over to make the new Queensgate Yard. The new yard cost $71 million and opened in 1980. Unlike recently constructed yards, such as Roseville or Livonia on the UP, Queensgate revolutionized railroad operations in Cincinnati rather than just providing minor improvements.

The scale of Queensgate Yard's impact can be understood by listing the other yards around greater Cincinnati that closed after it went into operation. First, five of the six yards north of Cincinnati's Union terminal, along Mill Creek, were covered over and closed as Queensgate was constructed. These were all Chessie yards, originally built by the B&O or C&O railroads. A Yard, Brighton Yard, Mill Creek Yard, and the Stock Yard made up the main B&O facilities in town, while Liberty Street Yard was a small C&O switching point. The Norfolk Southern yard at Gest Street is the only set of tracks from before 1980 that survives along the valley.

Elsewhere in Cincinnati, the C&O yard at Silver Grove closed in 1980. This contained an eastbound hump yard with a 26-track bowl and a westbound flat-switched yard with 14 tracks. The Louisville & Nashville yard at DeCoursey, much of which still lies derelict, closed in 1984. It had northbound and southbound hump yards, each with a 24-track bowl. The B&O closed Oakley Yard in 1987, while Conrail closed Undercliff Yard in 1980 and then their large hump yard at Sharon in 1987.

The complexity of Queensgate's network can be grasped by the fact that in 1980, there were 500 potential industry jobs from the yard. By the time of my first visit in 1995, this was down to 108 jobs, all within a 68-mile radius of the yard. This still represents a lot of local carload customers needing to classify cars for forwarding long-distance.

The yard contains eight receiving tracks, a 50-track bowl, and six departure tracks. It also features "three-point control," which was rare in 1980, present only at the West Colton and Barstow yards at that time. Three-point control means that retarders are placed beyond the hump in three positions, the last at the entrance to each bowl track. This system gives the finest possible control with traditional

Dire weather hampers those on the job in October 1995, but work goes on at Queensgate. This view was taken from Hopple Street looking south. It shows two trim jobs pulling cars out of the bowl. In the background is the lengthy Western Hills viaduct.

rail-brake retarders, although it is not as precise as the British Dowty retarder now used in Livonia and Roseville. Since 1980, little has changed at Queensgate.

Throughput of cars was said to be 3,200 when the yard opened. From the 1990s, it has remained fairly constant, hovering around 2,000 per day. Certainly it is possible to classify 2,500 cars in 24 hours, as inspection of the records indicated during my time in the tower, but average throughput is nearer 2,000. The official "staff briefing booklet" for new employees is called *2,100 Cars a Day, the Safe and Quality Way,* suggesting that this is the current ideal traffic burden for the complex.

To achieve this amount of classification, CSX employs 33 crews each day: 6 work the hump, 12 are needed at the north end of the yard for trim and pullout duties, and a further 12 are on industry jobs. The yard handles 57 scheduled merchandise trains every 24 hours, split almost in half between long-distance manifest trains and local industry jobs.

In 1995, manifest trains headed out for Ashland (1), Chicago (1), Columbus (1), Corbin and beyond (5), Detroit (3), Indianapolis (1), Louisville and beyond (6), Russell (2), Saginaw (1), St. Louis (4), Toledo (1), Dayton (1), and Willard (3). Since the merger with Conrail in 1999, several more eastern destinations have been added to this list, such as Selkirk Yard.

Queensgate is one of the most accessible yards in the country, with three excellent overpasses from which to view the complex. The best of these is the Western Hills viaduct, which crosses the southern approach to the hump and gives good views of the engine terminal, arrival tracks, and hump. Farther north, Hopple Street crosses the pullout area from the north end of the bowl, while farther south, the 8th Street viaduct crosses the entrance to the arrivals part of the yard.

This view of Queensgate was taken looking south from the Western Hills viaduct. In the distance is the old Cincinnati Union terminal. To its left is the CSX intermodal yard, while to the right in the far distance is NS's Gest Street Yard. CSX 1522 is one of the local industry jobs bringing intermodal cars from south of the Ohio River to the Cincinnati hub. The main tracks here see run-through traffic, such as unit coal trains and some intermodal traffic.

This view from the hump tower at Queensgate shows the three-point control system well. Each bowl track has a rail brake at its entrance.

On a gloriously sunny day in 1997, a CSX manifest arrives from the north, seen here passing the engine terminal from a position on the western end of a Western Hills viaduct. To the right of the picture, the hump approach road can be seen.

The vast double-hump yard at DeCoursey, 5 miles south of Cincinnati, didn't close until 1987. Even in 1995, many of the tracks were intact as this view from the southbound hump crest shows. The yard was used to store retired railroad cars awaiting the cutter's torch. Most were on the rails, but quite a few were stacked on spare ground as seen here. The northbound hump, which was older than the southbound hump, was almost completely covered by vegetation at the time of this visit in October 1995.

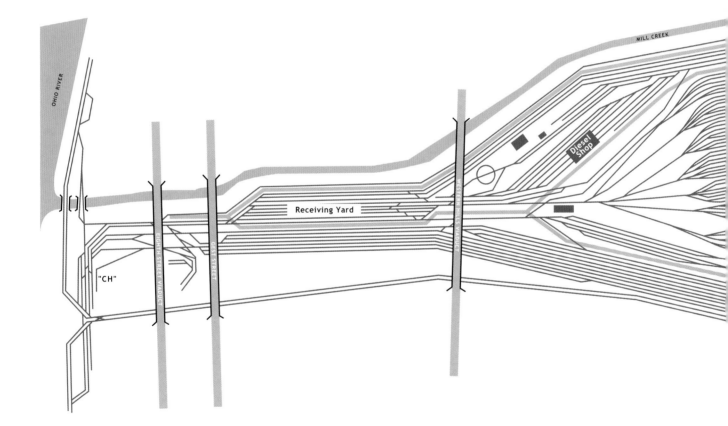

OHIO RIVER

"CH"

EIGHTH STREET VIADUCT

GEST STREET

Receiving Yard

WESTERN HILLS VIADUCT

Diesel Shop

MILL CREEK

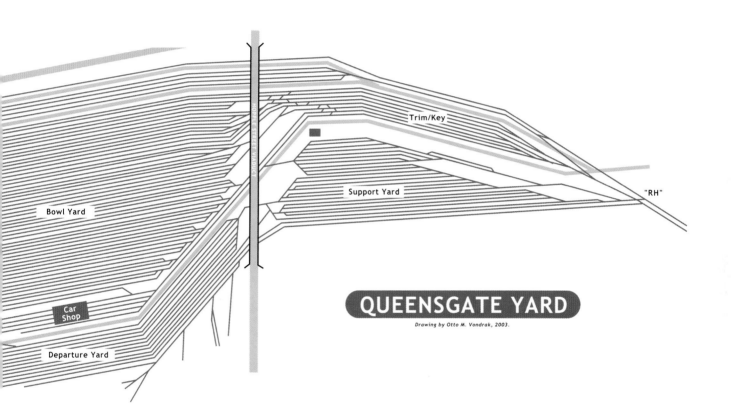

Bowl Yard

Car Shop

Departure Yard

HOPPLE STREET VIADUCT

Trim/Key

Support Yard

"RH"

QUEENSGATE YARD

*Drawing by Otto M. Vondrak, 2003.*

Seaboard Systems opened Rice Yard in 1978 and named it after the erstwhile president of the Atlantic Coast Line Railroad, W. Thomas Rice. The yard is the largest owned by the CSX and cost $56 million to build. It lies southwest of downtown Waycross. From small beginnings in the late 1800s, when 36 acres of land were purchased for railroad tracks, the site has expanded to 850 acres and more than 150 miles of track. The yard and associated engine house and shops employ 1,200 people.

The physical layout of the yard includes 12 receiving tracks, which can hold up to 200 cars each. These lead over a dual hump to a 64-track bowl. The hump was designed to allow arrivals to be humped simultaneously, but this no longer happens. Too many individual classifications are needed on one arrival, which leads to conflicting movements if two trains are running over the hump simultaneously. The yard has 14 departure tracks, 10 for northbound trains and 4 for southbound traffic. Add to this a 10-track local yard and the total is standing room for 8,500 cars.

The complex is designed to classify 2,900 cars daily over the hump and often reaches this target. During my visit in 1999, 2,719 cars had been classified in the previous 24 hours. There were 1,238 cars in the receiving tracks, 1,219 in the bowl, and 872 standing in the departure tracks. Pressure often mounts, because the bowl and departure yard fill if power to remove trains from the yard is insufficient—the yard staff calls this the "choke point."

Waycross is unusual, in that it sees little run-through or unit-train traffic. It has 25 departures each day. Only four trains are locals; the rest are long-haul manifest trains, destined for CSX yards as far away as Selkirk and Chicago (Barr Yard). Only two or three trains each day bypass the hump at Rice.

Rice Yard has its own engine house and locomotive service facility, which is where railroad workers do running repairs, refueling, and sanding on locomotives that arrive with the daily diet of 25 manifest freights. As well as housing these facilities, Rice Yard is home to one of CSX's largest

A CSX yard slug pulls cars out from the south end of the Rice Yard classification bowl in 1999. Behind lie the classification tracks, with the hump crest just visible in the distance.

A view from the pullout tower at the south of the Waycross complex shows the bowl in the center of the image. To the left are the northbound departure tracks, while the lead to the four southbound departure tracks can just be seen on the right.

locomotive repair facilities, which is located to the north of the yard, within a mile of downtown Waycross. Everything from repainting to total rebuilding of locomotives takes place here.

Unfortunately, neither the workshops nor the yard at Rice are readily viewed from a public place. The yard lies along U.S. Highway 82. A left turn on Oklahoma Avenue leads to the main yard office, but this is a private road. There is also access to the south end of the yard, along Hamilton Avenue and South Road, both of which are on CSXT property.

On a very wet and dull morning in 1999, the bowl at Rice Yard is seen full of 1,219 cars. CSX slug 2422 with an auxiliary power unit descends into the bowl to trim some of the classification tracks where cars have stopped short of the correct position.

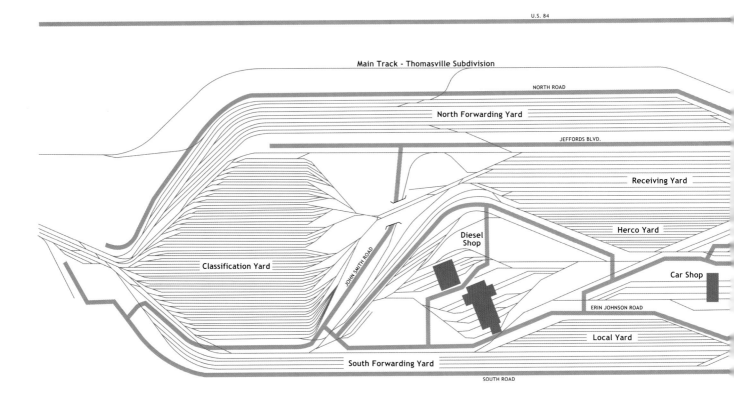

U.S. 84

Main Track - Thomasville Subdivision

NORTH ROAD

North Forwarding Yard

JEFFORDS BLVD.

Receiving Yard

Herco Yard

Diesel Shop

Car Shop

Classification Yard

JOHN SMITH ROAD

ERIN JOHNSON ROAD

Local Yard

South Forwarding Yard

SOUTH ROAD

This busy view with four layers of CSX power was taken from Rice Yard's "A Tower." CSX 2422 is on the hump while its sister locomotive, No. 7011, has just been released from an arrival and is passing under the hump to the servicing facility. CSX 1166 and 5840 are both standing on the servicing tracks, which lie adjacent to the main hump.

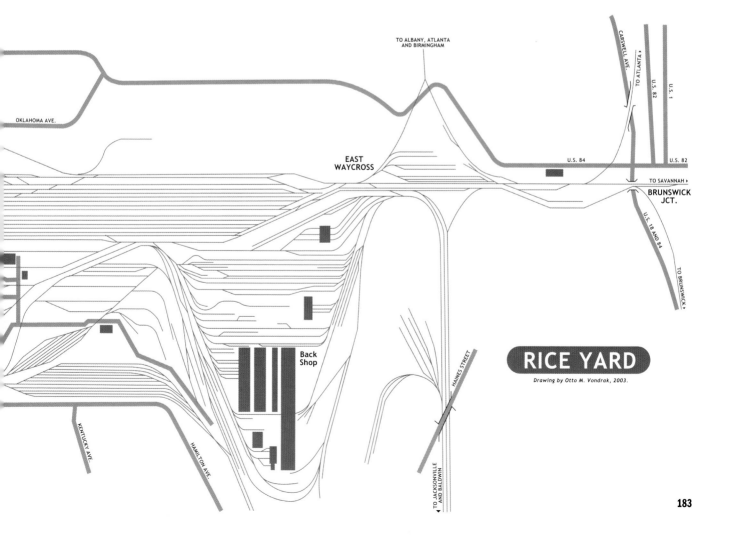

RICE YARD

*Drawing by Otto M. Vondrak, 2003.*

# Osborn Yard—Louisville, Kentucky

Seaboard Systems opened Osborn Yard in 1977, replacing a smaller L&N yard just to the north. The yard has 22 reception tracks, 12 of which are 8,000 feet long. The other 10 are only 2,300 feet and are designed to accommodate industry locals with 30 or 40 cars. The hump leads to a 48-track bowl and two sets of eight departure tracks, again all around 8,000 feet in length. The hump has modern "real-time" speed indicators that monitor cars as they descend the hump. During my visit in 1998, the yard was handling 500 to 600 cars a shift over the hump.

The yard lies south of Louisville, to the west of the international airport. Views of the yard from public places are poor, but much of the complex can be seen, even if not photographed, by driving south along Crittenden Drive and then turning right along Grade Lane.

Dawn at Osborn Yard in May 1998. The classification bowl is quiet as shifts change in the hump tower. The departure tracks lie to the right and left of the main bowl.

Two hump slugs with auxiliary power units stand on the hump approach at Osborn Yard. Behind them are the reception tracks; to the left is the engine house.

The yardmaster taking the 6:00 A.M. shift settles into his chair in front of the switches that control access to the bowl tracks at Osborn. The yard floodlights are still on, but soon it will be daylight and cars will start to roll over the hump.

The L&N Railroad opened Radnor Yard, one of the largest yards on CSX, in 1954. It has standing room for 7,905 cars and rates as one of the top three yards on CSX, along with Queensgate and Waycross. The 13 receiving tracks feed a 56-track classification bowl. During my visit in 1998, the yard was classifying between 1,700 and 2,100 cars each day over the hump.

The yard is 4 miles south of downtown Nashville. From an excellent overpass to the south of the classification bowl, both receiving tracks and the hump can be observed. This is called Harding Place, which is an exit from I-65.

Cars roll into the bowl at Radnor Yard at sunset on a day in October 1998. The cars are part of a manifest that arrived earlier in the day from the massive Clearing Yard in Chicago.

This view from Harding Place, looking north, shows that all of Radnor's tracks are full. A double-stack run-through passes cars being humped. On the right, cars are being pulled out into the hump approach for re-humping. This location is busy throughout the day.

CP boxcars roll through the retarders behind a CSX TOFC train about to depart southbound. This view was also taken from Harding Place with a long lens.

The Louisville & Nashville opened Tilford Yard in 1957 at a cost of $11 million. When new, it had a relatively small classification bowl, with just 24 classification tracks. The whole complex had capacity to accommodate only 2,141 cars.

The yard has been expanded since then and now has a 40-track bowl fed by eight long arrival roads and supported by nine departure tracks. During my visit in 1998, the hump classified 1,300 cars a day, but the terminal itself was far busier than this. One hundred trains per day passed through the terminal, which is a bit of a bottleneck for CSX, and the mainline past the yard is busy.

The yard lies in a valley alongside the NS facility at Inman, approximately 5 miles northwest of downtown Atlanta. Marietta Road offers excellent views of the arrival and departure tracks as well as of the CSX mainline through Atlanta. If you continue north along Marietta Road, you can see the hump bowl down in the valley, on the left.

The 40-track bowl at Tilford is seen here from the hump tower in 1998. The central three fans of tracks contain the original 24 tracks that were installed in 1957, when the yard was opened.

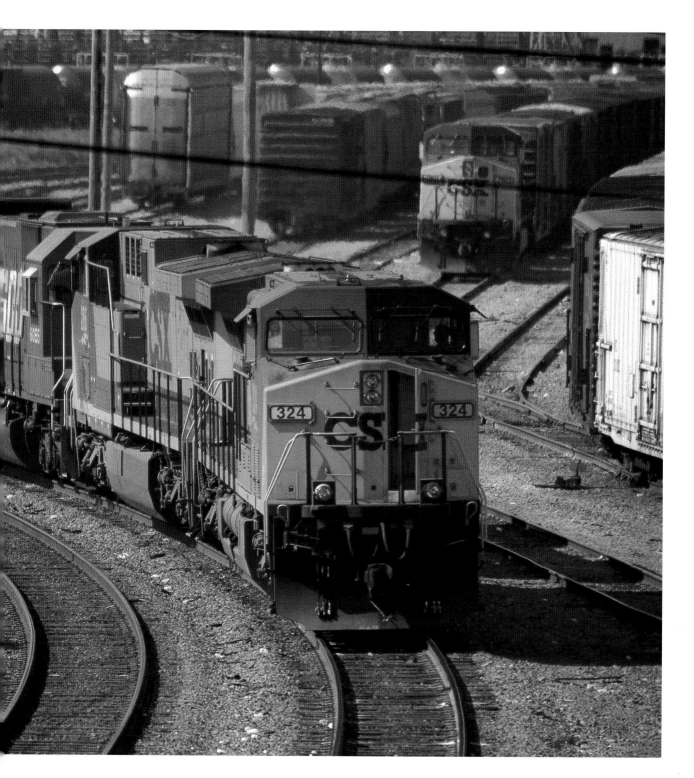

A run-through manifest heading south passes the departure tracks at Tilford Yard. Views to the north and south from Marieta Road are excellent, with plenty of opportunities for photography.

The Louisville & Nashville opened Boyles Yard in 1958. The yard, which cost $10 million to build, has standing room for 6,151 cars and a total of 122 tracks stretching more than 95 miles. Nine receiving tracks lead to a 40-track bowl. The 12 departure tracks lie along the western edge of the bowl. In addition to these tracks, a separate south yard handles local traffic and has a large engine house. During my visit in 1998, the yard was classifying 1,100 cars each day over the hump, with another 1,100 cars passing through each day on run-through freights.

The yard is hard to find, even with a street plan of Birmingham. It lies just west of Birmingham Municipal Airport and can be found by driving north along Vanderbilt Road. A left turn on Cedar Street leads to Seaboard Road, which runs the length of the yard for 4 miles. There are no convenient overpasses, and most views of the yard are from railroad property.

The 40-track bowl at Boyles is identical in layout to the other L&N yard at Tilford. This view was taken as cars descended the hump during one evening in 1998.

The yard at Hamlet owes its existence to the Seaboard and Atlantic Coast Lines Railroad, which opened it in 1954. It was built on a greenfield site 5 miles north of Hamlet and cost $8 million. At the time of construction, there was debate about the best location for a hump yard in the area. Many railroaders felt that nearby Pembroke would have been a more natural choice for the new yard. Perhaps the cost of land swayed the choice in favor of Hamlet.

The 10 receiving tracks were built, leading to a 58-track bowl and 11 departure roads. The bowl tracks are relatively short in Hamlet, holding 22 to 57 cars. The whole complex has room for 5,030 cars. During 1999, the yard was handling 600 cars per shift over the hump. Its situation along Route 177, 5 miles north of Hamlet, is in open countryside but provides no convenient public places from which to observe the yard.

This view is from the hump tower at Hamlet, looking toward the receiving tracks. Being pushed over the hump are some cars from an 81-car manifest that had arrived earlier in the morning from Raleigh.

This view from the hump tower at Hamlet shows the 58-track classification bowl. Those who are observant will spot a stretch of green land at either edge of the bowl. Seaboard allowed space for another 22 classification tracks when the yard was built in 1954. These have never been added, leaving some spare land in the complex.

A quiet moment in Hamlet tower. Hmm . . . where do those cars go?

The yard at Cumberland is of B&O parentage and is squeezed into the valley floor southeast of downtown Cumberland. It opened in 1960. The capital project to build a push-button hump yard here cost $10 million. The westbound yard is the hump facility at Cumberland, with smaller, adjacent yards handling through hopper trains and eastbound traffic.

Eight receiving tracks lead over the hump to a 30-track bowl, which also has three additional tracks for "bad order" cars. These three short tracks lead directly into the yard's car repair facility. The yard has no departure tracks as such, and manifest freights tend to be assembled in bowl tracks 1 to 5, which are more than 100 cars long. This leads to some complex switching at the western end of the bowl, with pullout of cars and building of trains all taking place in the bowl tracks.

The old eastbound yard has been altered considerably over the years and now has five long loops to accommodate unit coal trains that can undergo inspection and power changes in the yard. The old eastbound classification bowl contains an assortment of 27 more tracks, some "stub ended." In addition, the cramped valley floor also has room for a large locomotive shop and roundhouse.

The 1999 consolidation of CSX with parts of Conrail greatly increased traffic through Cumberland, which was one of the points on the CSX system that saw marked congestion after the merger. During my visit in 1999, 1,400 cars each day were being handled over the hump, as well as a large volume of run-through traffic.

Access to the yard is quite good, with an overpass on Mexico Farms Road at the eastern end of the receiving tracks and several side roads in the area, which give views of the receiving yard. Route 51 runs along the valley floor and close to the yard all the way into Cumberland. It contains several parking spots from which the hump and bowl can be observed. At the western end of the complex, parking spots either side of the line off Virginia Avenue give good views along the mainline and back toward the bowl.

At the Baltimore end of the Cumberland receiving yard, two CSX yard slugs await hump duties. A lash-up of Conrail diesels has just arrived from the west with a manifest for classification.

The classification bowl at Cumberland is seen from the hump tower in 1999. In the distance to the left is the car repair shop and, farther left, are the tracks that remain from the eastbound bowl.

This view was taken from Virginia Avenue and shows a CSX manifest arriving from the west in Cumberland. Tracks here are often choked with busy run-through traffic and pullout work from the westbound classification bowl.

The complex at Willard is perhaps the single place on the CSX network most changed by the Conrail takeover in 1999. Willard was a B&O yard, built in 1947, and an integral part of the route from Baltimore and Washington over Sandpatch to Chicago and the West. Since the Conrail acquisition, it has become an exceptionally busy junction, because the new CSX line from Selkirk, Buffalo, and Cleveland joins the old B&O mainline just east of Willard Yard. Up to 90 trains daily pass the yard, making it one of the busiest spots on the U.S. railroad network.

The yard has had two separate hump yards since 1947. The eastbound yard is the larger of the two, with eight receiving tracks leading to a 32-track bowl. As was typical in a 1940s-era yard, these bowl tracks were short, many holding as few as 20 cars. Since the merger with Conrail, two-thirds have been doubled in length, to help classify the longer manifest trains of the twenty-first century.

The westbound bowl has nine receiving tracks and 20 classification tracks; again, over half of these were lengthened in a massive 1998 to 1999 improvement program. Both humps can handle 800 cars per day, but run-through traffic marks this yard as one of the busiest in the United States. The biggest change of the recent rebuild is the addition of a run-through yard for 1,000-mile inspection and re-crewing of through freights. Eight new 8,000-foot to 10,000-foot tracks have been added on the perimeter of the yard, to ease congestion along this Ohio racetrack.

The yard lies on the edge of the small Ohio town of Willard and has several places to catch the action, including an excellent overpass to the east of the yard complex. There is plenty of open country around the yard and grade crossings to the east and west of the yard.

The 1940s-era retarders of Willard's westbound hump are seen here from the hump crest in 1999. The 20-track bowl stretches away in the distance.

The slogan on the westbound hump tower says it all: "More Trains - No Peace." The old B&O switching gear is still in use at Willard, as seen from this ancient hump panel. From a sleepy 1940s hump yard in danger of closure, Willard has been transformed by the Conrail merger into the busiest spot on CSXT.

East of Willard Yard, trains line up to make it onto the eastbound mainline to Washington and New York.

This aerial view of the Willard complex was taken by one of the railroaders at the yard during the 1999 rebuild. Looking from the east toward the west, the separate classification yards can be seen, as well as the new run-through tracks to the north of the old yards

Raceland Yard (also known as Fitzpatrick Yard) is on the southern banks of the Ohio River in Russell, Kentucky. Two large sets of sidings are the remnants of two parallel hump systems, one for coal and one for manifests. The yard dates back to the 1800s and has been expanded and refined, largely under C&O ownership in the 1950s and 1960s. Since 1990, both humps have closed, although the yard remains busy with unit coal traffic.

The complex in Russell is unusual in that it contained two parallel hump yards, both designed to classify traffic running west. The yard nearest the Ohio River was exclusively for coal traffic and had a 51-track bowl. Hump operations here were abandoned in 1995, as most Kentucky coal moved as unit trains to the west and then north to Toledo. In addition, coal traveled in barges along the Ohio River to five major power plants on the way to Cincinnati. These changes greatly reduced carload coal traffic, and the hump closed.

The second hump yard, for manifest trains, opened in 1959 at a cost of $4.8 million. It boasted a 32-track bowl and 36 tracks each for arrival, departure, and run-through manifest trains. A reorganization of CSX carload services led to the 1991 closure of the hump in the manifest yard.

Today, the yard is still busy with up to 50 run-through services each day, mainly in the form of unit coal traffic. There are no easy public viewing places for the yard, although the complex can be glimpsed from the main road between Raceland and Ashland.

Two unit coal empties stand in the run-through tracks on the southern perimeter of Russell Yard on an extremely gloomy day in April 1997. By 1997, the complex certainly had an air of dereliction—it was a pale reflection of the yard that had boasted in the 1950s of being one of the biggest in the world.

# Walbridge Yard—Toledo, Ohio

After Russell Yard in Kentucky, this was the second largest yard on the C&O Railroad. It was a big hump yard, with eight receiving tracks leading to a 68-track classification bowl. It had more than 40 additional tracks, mainly for southbound classification.

In the early 1990s, CSX removed the hump and tore up the classification bowl. Carload traffic still uses the remains of the receiving yard and the old eastbound flat-switched yard. A steady stream of unit coal trains passes on their way to the Toledo docks. Since the merger with Conrail in 1999, much carload traffic has been moved to the neighboring Stanley Yard, and the days are probably numbered for the site at Walbridge.

Access to the yard is quite good, as it lies in open country to the south of Toledo. Like Stanley Yard, Walbridge can be seen looking north from Route 795 and also (less well) looking north from the Ohio Turnpike. Luckey Road and Drouilard Road run north from Route 795 on either side of Walbridge. Walbridge Road crosses the north of the complex on a flat crossing.

The CSX mainline at Walbridge is still busy with coal and manifest traffic. Two trains are seen passing here at Walbridge Road.

The eastbound yard at Walbridge is still busy with carload switching. In the background, Route 795 can be seen crossing the yard.

The Norfolk Southern (NS) Railroad is a product of the 1982 merger of the Southern Railroad and Norfolk & Western Railroad. Most of the yards on the modern-day NS—seven of them—owe their existence to the ex–Southern Railroad half of the partnership. Two yards originate from the Norfolk Western: the most modern yard on the network, at Bellevue, and perhaps the most famous, Shaffers Crossing, at Roanoke. In addition, NS took over 58 percent of Conrail in the 1998 Conrail breakup; part of the assets include yards at Allentown, Columbus, Conway, and Elkhart.

Three other yards owned by NS deserve mention. First is the ex-Pennsylvania yard at Enola, dealt with in detail in the Conrail section of this book. In 2002, NS reopened part of Enola for classification.

A second yard, rarely mentioned in the railway press, is the hump yard at Lambert's Point, Virginia. The coal yards here are designed mainly to handle trans-shipment of 100-plus car unit coal trains into bulk-carrying ships bound for Europe and Asia. Within the complex at Lambert's Point is a discrete hump yard for empty coal cars. In the middle of more than 100 tracks for unit trains nestles a 24-track bowl, with retarders to control the return of cars from Pier Six. The yard is completely inaccessible, except from the air.

The final NS yard is the largest flat yard in the United States, in Decatur, Georgia. Most large yards employ hump technology. Others, such as those at Toledo Docks, Alliance, or Lambert's Point, are designed almost exclusively for unit trains. There are, however, one or two large flat-switched yards. CSX has one at Barr in southern Chicago, but the biggest is Decatur.

An NS switcher pulls cars out of the eastbound classification tracks at Decatur, Georgia, to build a manifest for Detroit. At this writing, the Decatur facility was the largest flat yard in the United States. This train was eventually made up of 186 cars and weighed 8,000 tons.

Decatur has 38 eastbound and 48 westbound classification tracks, some long enough to accommodate 150 cars. During a visit in 1995, the yard was classifying more than 3,000 cars a day as well as handling significant run-through traffic. Twenty-two daily manifests were built in the yards at Decatur in 1995, with long-distance trains to Detroit, Roanoke, Bellevue, Kansas City, St. Louis, Sheffield, and Norfolk. The yard in Decatur is viewed well from a bridge at the western end of the complex.

From the yard tower at the east end of the Decatur complex, a run-through freight from Detroit to St. Louis passes the yard. The Road Railer is carrying parts for the auto industry.

# Sevier Yard—Knoxville, Tennessee

Sevier Yard is the first modern hump yard that Southern Railroad built; it opened in 1951 at a cost of $4 million. The yard was Southern Railroad's first attempt to deal with congestion problems in its terminals in the 1950s as railroad traffic grew in the South. Especially prominent was the expansion of government manufacturing plants and military production in the southern states. The Southern Railroad therefore built two new push-button hump yards in Knoxville and Birmingham, as well as expanding and improving its yards in Atlanta and Chattanooga.

The land 8 miles east of Knoxville had held two classification yards, one for eastbound traffic and one for westbound. Neither had any forwarding tracks—trains moved directly from the classification tracks. This was possible because of a limited number of classification options: four eastbound and six westbound. When it opened in 1951, the yard had 30 arrivals and 30 departures every day. It was not unusual to have 3,000 to 3,500 cars arrive every day. The hump at the new automated yard classified 2,000 of these, on average.

The yard has 12 receiving tracks. Six are restricted to between 67 and 75 40-foot boxcars, while the other six can handle between 145 and 153 arriving cars. The hump leads to a 46-track bowl; the yard has 11 departure tracks.

This view from the hump tower at Sevier Yard shows the classification bowl. The primary retarder is in need of some running repairs, bringing a temporary halt to classification and time for a quick coffee in the hump tower.

During my visit in 1998, the yard was classifying 1,500 cars each day over the hump. Access is poor, but the yard can be found by traveling east out of Knoxville on Rutledge Pike. This road crosses the NS mainline into the yard, and an immediate right turn onto Old Rutledge Pike leads you along the northern edge of the yard.

Looking west from the hump tower at Knoxville shows the arrival tracks. The long 100-plus car tracks are on the left; shorter tracks for industry locals and small manifests are on the right.

Opened in 1952, Norris Yard is now one of the largest hump yards on the NS. It has overtaken Inman in Atlanta, where the hump has been closed and much of the facility is used by intermodal traffic, but it lags behind DeButts Yard in Chattanooga. The 12 arrival tracks lead into a 56-track bowl, and car throughput was around 1,600 per day during my visit in 1998. The yard lies on the northeastern outskirts of Birmingham. Access for the railfan is poor. For one traveling out of Birmingham on Ruffner Road, the facility can be glimpsed on the right.

It's 6:00 A.M. one summer morning, and as luck would have it, a Southern steel coil carrier descends the hump at Southern's largest yard, Norris.

The view from the hump tower shows the bowl at Norris Yard, with seven fans of eight tracks in perfect symmetry.

DeButts Yard is the busiest on NS, handling 2,500 cars every day over the hump. Not only that, but the yard is perhaps the most accessible on NS and is a great place to watch trains, as the CSX mainline skirts its southern boundary. Southern Railroad opened the yard in 1955 at a cost of $12 million. It has 12 receiving tracks, a 60-track classification bowl, and 11 departure roads. The yard contains 100 miles of track, with room for 6,300 cars.

Three conveniently situated overpasses permit viewing the yard. At the western end, Meharry Drive (Route 153) crosses the entrance to the receiving tracks. The Jersey Pike crosses the yard at the eastern end of the receiving yard. Reid Road crosses the eastern end of the whole complex as well as the CSX mainline. All three bridges give good views of action in the yard.

A manifest arrives in DeButts' receiving tracks from the east and is photographed from Meharry Drive. On the right are NS and CSX run-through tracks, which at this moment have a unit coal train on them with SP power on the rear.

The yard towers in Knoxville, Birmingham, and Chattanooga are of identical design. Here, cars approach the hump at DeButts in October 1998.

The 60-track bowl at DeButts is now the largest on NS, since the tracks at Atlanta's Inman yard have been rearranged for container traffic. After the diversion of traffic from Inman Yard in 1993, the hump at DeButts has become much busier.

The view from the Jersey Pike shows the hump in the distance. An NS yard switcher with auxiliary power unit has almost completed the classification of 150 cars and will then return to the other end of the receiving tracks, to start propelling another manifest over the hump.

Cars are pulled out from the bowl to be placed in the departure tracks on the right. This view is from Reid Road and also shows the CSX mainline on the left.

Inman was the largest yard that NS inherited from the Southern Railroad in 1982. It opened in 1957, with space for 7,800 cars on its tracks. Since the 1950s, NS has added an intermodal hump yard and a rail welding plant. By the 1980s, the yard had room for more than 10,000 cars, putting it in the same league as famous northeastern yards such as Enola and Conway.

In the 1980s, the layout at Inman included a 16-track receiving yard for inbound trains and a single-track hump leading to a 65-track classification bowl. "Trim jobs" at the north end of the yard would pull cars from the classification bowl and propel them into one of 16 departure tracks along the west side of the complex. There was also a 10-track local yard at the north end of the bowl.

To the north of the receiving yard lay the intermodal hump, with 20 classification tracks and two loading tracks. In addition, the yard complex had car shops, an engine house, and a rail welding plant, which produced most of the rail on the NS. In 1992, a typical day saw 56 manifest trains terminate or originate at Inman and more than 2,500 cars classified on the hump.

Inman's geographical location and the intermodal revolution spelled the end for the hump at Inman and for much of its classification work. NS calculated that savings could be made and transit times improved if trains bypassed Inman in favor of classification at other yards. Inman lies at the center of six other major NS yards: Brosnan, Linwood, Chattanooga, Knoxville, Birmingham, and Sheffield. By pre-blocking carloads at these yards to bypass Atlanta, residual carload traffic for the greater Atlanta area could be handled at a scaled-down Inman as well as at local yards at East Point and Chamblee.

These diversions were put in place in 1993. This allowed NS to expand the intermodal facility at Inman from 39 to 65 acres and to close the intermodal hump in favor of more pavement for trucks. NS also removed eight of the 16 receiving tracks in favor of more intermodal space. The classification bowl remains in place but the retarders have been removed, and the bowl tracks are increasingly filled with TOFC and COFC traffic.

Marietta Road crosses the receiving tracks of Inman, while Perry Boulevard runs along the western edge of the complex.

Kansas City Southern units await departure with an intermodal train to Shreveport, Louisiana. The train is standing in one of the eight remaining receiving tracks at Inman and is viewed from the Marietta Road overpass.

The bowl at Inman was full of container traffic by the time of my visit in 1998. Two retarders were still in position, although control systems from the tower to them had been disconnected.

The yard at Muscle Shoals, near Sheffield, opened in 1973. It was built to address congestion in the old Sheffield Yard and also to relieve overcrowding at Forrest Yard, Memphis. This is the smallest hump yard on the NS, with six receiving tracks leading over a single-track hump to a 32-track classification bowl. The yard handles 300 to 400 cars per shift. The yard lies in open country east of Muscle Shoals and can be seen from both Thoroughfare Road and Middle Road.

The bowl at Sheffield Yard, as seen from the hump tower in 1998.

A country lane passes the eastern end of the bowl at Sheffield. Two NS switchers are on trim jobs, pulling out cars from the bowl.

# Brosnan Yard—Macon, Georgia

Completed in 1967, this was the fifth large push-button hump yard the Southern Railroad built. It has become much busier since the end of classification at Inman. It has 10 receiving tracks leading to a 50-track bowl and is the most southerly yard on NS. The yard lies in woodland to the south of Macon and has no easy access points from which to view it.

## Sample Train Plan for Brosnan Yard in February 1996

| TRAIN NUMBER | TIME at MACON | FROM | TO |
|---|---|---|---|
| 419 | 0200 | Macon | Albany |
| 335 | 0230–0330 | Savannah | Birmingham |
| 239 | 0345–0430 | St. Louis | Bowden |
| 229 | 0345–0350 | Cincinnati | Bowden |
| 199 | 0400–1000 | Valdosta | Birmingham |
| 192 | 0400–1730 | Sheffield | Nixon |
| 161 | 0600 | Chattanooga | Macon |
| 140 | 0600 | Macon | Knoxville |
| 230 | 0730–0840 | Jacksonville | Atlanta |
| 198 | 0900–1201 | Birmingham | Valdosta |
| 436 | 0930 | Macon | Savannah |
| 321 | 1155–1600 | Chattanooga | Bowden |
| 191 | 2230–0800 | Nixon | Sheffield |
| 634 | 1500 | Macon | Tennille |
| 118 | 1600 | Macon | Linwood |
| 119 | 1600 | Linwood | Macon |
| 160 | 1830 | Macon | Louisville |
| 312 | 1830 | Brunswick | Macon |
| 311 | 1900 | Macon | Brunswick |
| 435 | 1925 | Savannah | Macon |
| 330 | 1945 | Bowden | Macon |
| 418 | 2000 | Albany | Macon |
| 210 | 2020–2120 | Miami | Atlanta |
| 336 | 2115–2215 | Birmingham | Savannah |
| 688 | 2245–2345 | Tennille | Chattanooga |
| 322 | 2345–1230 | Jacksonville | Chattanooga |

ABOVE: The bowl at Brosnan Yard is seen here from the tower, looking north. Since the closure of Inman, the yard handles up to 1,500 cars a day.
BELOW: The view south from the tower shows Brosnan's 10 receiving tracks. On this occasion they are all empty. *Both photos Carl Ardrey*

S pencer Yard, opened in 1979, is the seventh and last built by the Southern Railroad. It is roughly halfway between Atlanta and Washington, on a 600-mile stretch that was previously without any significant hump yard. It was built 8 miles north of Spencer, North Carolina, and allowed switching to be phased out at the old Spencer flat yard. It also allowed reduced classification at the yards in Greensboro, Lynchburg, and Asheville. The site chosen was a greenfield site, free from road crossings. As a result, it is difficult to observe the yard except from railroad property.

The yard is 4.5 miles long and covers 376 acres. The receiving yard has eight tracks, varying in length from 116 cars to 169 (based on a 55-foot boxcar). A single-track hump leads to a 46-track bowl, where the tracks vary from 36 to 56 boxcars. The forwarding or departure yard has eight tracks, varying in length from 101 to 164 boxcars. In all, the yard has room for nearly 5,000 cars on 65 miles of track.

Interestingly, the rail in the classification bowl is lighter, at 100 pounds per foot, than rail elsewhere in the yard, which is 132 pounds per foot so that it can accommodate heavier usage. Traffic at the yard consists of 28 manifests made up or broken down daily as well as several locals. Eight daily intermodal trains bypass the yard.

ABOVE: Looking back from the hump tower, the eight-track arrival yard is visible. On the right is the large engine house built to service the yard. RIGHT: Spencer Yard's 46-track bowl is seen from the hump tower. On the right of the bowl is space for four more classification tracks that have never been added. *Both photos Carl Ardrey*

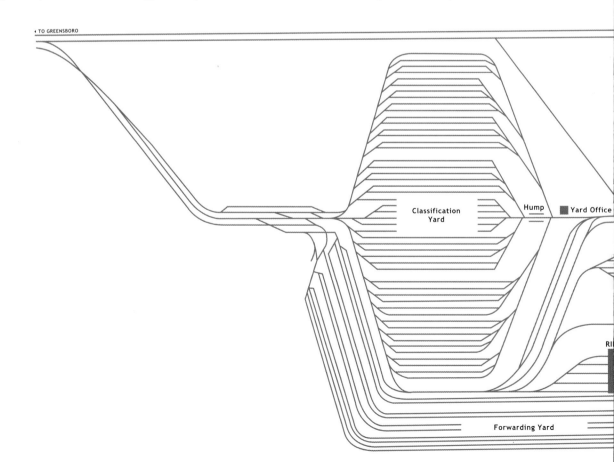

‹ TO GREENSBORO

Classification Yard

Hump

Yard Office

Forwarding Yard

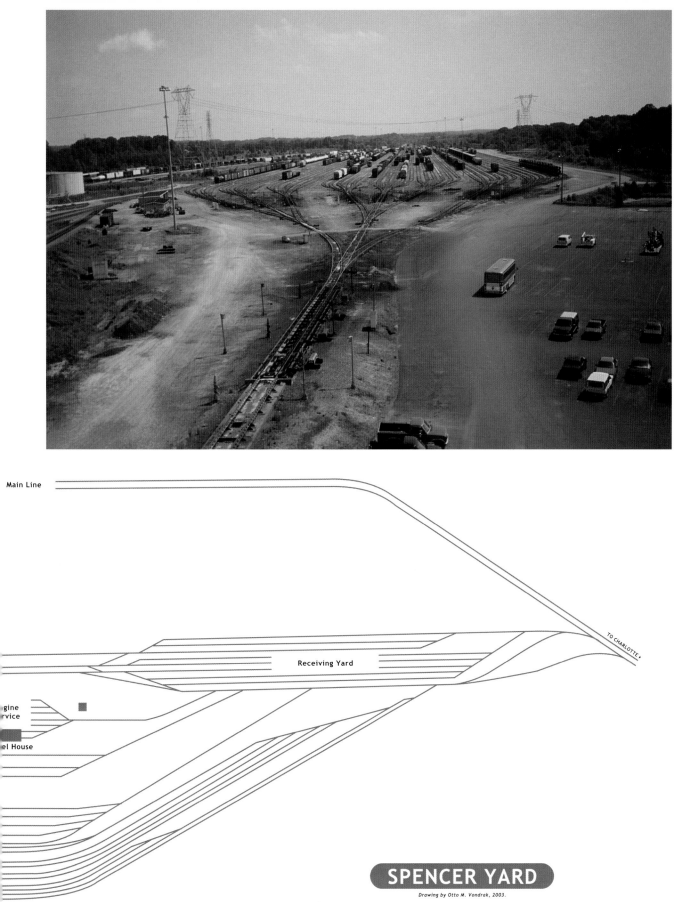

Main Line

TO CHARLOTTE ▶

Receiving Yard

...gine
...rvice

...el House

SPENCER YARD

*Drawing by Otto M. Vondrak, 2003.*

Shaffers Crossing is a 1950s hump yard. The location was made famous by O. Winston Link and his photos of the end of steam on the Norfolk & Western Railroad. Today, the hump yard is mainly bypassed by unit coal trains, which run through Roanoke on a bypass line to the south of the yard and the passenger depot. The yard lies just east of downtown and offers several convenient public places to watch traffic, including an overpass at the east of the complex.

The yard has 20 receiving tracks, a double-track hump, and 55 classification tracks. There are 16 departure tracks as well as 10 staging sidings for run-through trains. During my visit in 1997, the hump classified only 900 cars a day, although thousands more passed through the Roanoke terminal area, mainly in the form of unit coal trains.

A footbridge from the public road extends over the hump at Roanoke. This view, taken from the footbridge, shows the dual-track hump and the 1950s classification bowl.

Typical of Shaffers Crossing trains, this unit coal train is bypassing the hump yard as it makes its way east to Lambert's Point in April 1997.

The engine house at Shaffers Crossing achieved legendary status in the 1950s. Unfortunately, the modern rebuild for diesel maintenance is less atmospheric but is still busy with repairs to NS units.

Bellevue opened in 1982 and, along with Roanoke, is one of only two hump yards left on the Norfolk & Western (N&W) used for manifest traffic. The yard is on one of the busiest stretches of line on the NS and became busier after the merger with Conrail in 1998. The yard has clearly been constructed with a view to expansion, because its 42-track classification bowl occupies less than 50 percent of the space available for classification tracks. It could be expanded to more than 80 tracks if traffic demanded. There are 11 receiving tracks, plus 6 westbound and 4 eastbound departure tracks.

At the western end of the modern hump yard are two smaller yards that predate the hump yard. The west yard has 20 tracks, some of which have been partially removed to make way for a rail welding yard. The east yard has 23 tracks. Both these yards handle local traffic. A large engine house adjacent to the main hump services 1,500 units every month.

Traffic at the yard is around 1,400 cars per day. Of the 85 to 100 trains that pass Bellevue, 65 stop for remarshaling of some sort. About 40 will be classified over the hump. This activity can be viewed from a conveniently located overpass at the eastern end of the complex. Unfortunately, most trains arrive from the west, with lines coming in from Sandusky, Toledo, Fort Wayne, Portsmouth, and Brewster. They pull into the reception yard and are humped here as opposed to departing and running along the route to the east.

This view from the Bellevue hump tower shows the classification bowl, eccentrically located on the northern half of the land allocated for track.

RIGHT: This official NS aerial photo shows even more clearly the bowl at Bellevue and gives the impression of an unfinished yard.

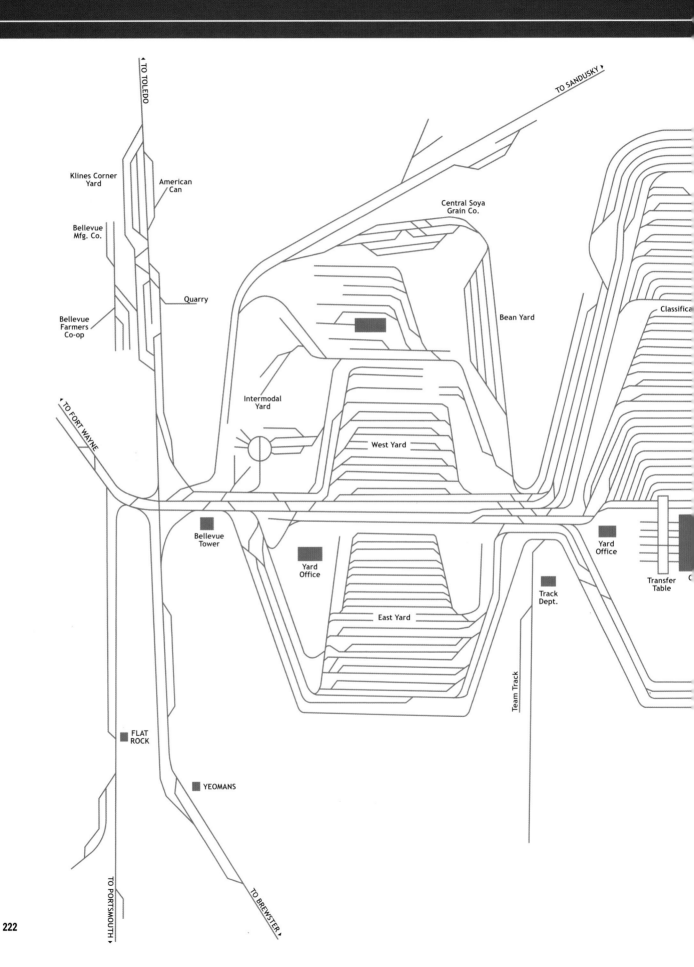

TO TOLEDO

TO SANDUSKY

Klines Corner
Yard

American
Can

Central Soya
Grain Co.

Bellevue
Mfg. Co.

Quarry

Bean Yard

Classifica

Bellevue
Farmers
Co-op

TO FORT WAYNE

Intermodal
Yard

West Yard

Bellevue
Tower

Yard
Office

Yard
Office

East Yard

Track
Dept.

Transfer
Table

Team Track

FLAT
ROCK

YEOMANS

TO PORTSMOUTH

TO BREWSTER

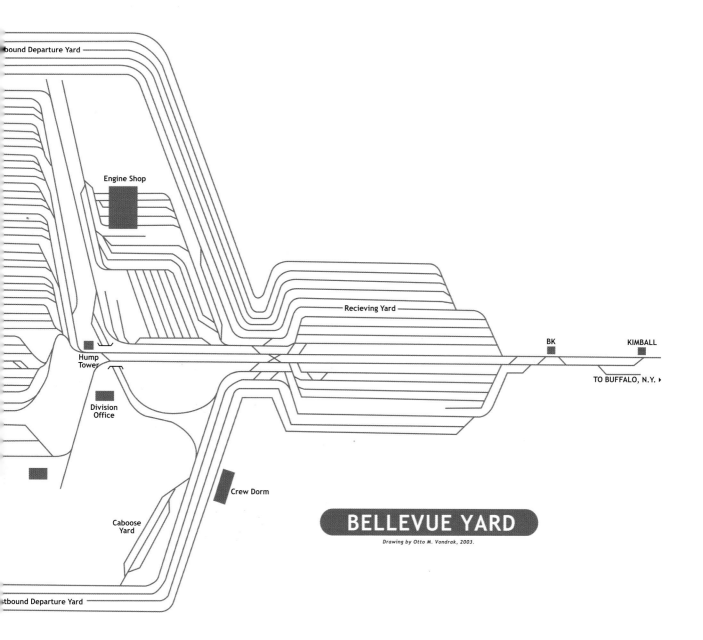

bound Departure Yard

Engine Shop

Recieving Yard

BK

KIMBALL

Hump
Tower

TO BUFFALO, N.Y. ▸

Division
Office

Crew Dorm

Caboose
Yard

**BELLEVUE YARD**

*Drawing by Otto M. Vondrak, 2003.*

tbound Departure Yard

Many other classification yards have not been described in detail in this book. Many are long gone, the result of mergers and a reduction in carload traffic. The yard at Sayre in Pennsylvania, so long the center for manifest traffic on the Lehigh Valley, and the yard at Silvis that served the Rock Island Line have been consigned to the history books.

Perhaps the most dramatic "disappearance" of a yard during the 14 years I have been researching this book is the massive Potomac Yard in Alexandria. The Richmond, Fredericksburg & Potomac Railroad owned this yard and closed it because of a loss of interchange traffic between southern railroads and Conrail. Northbound and southbound hump yards covered 520 acres and contained 136 miles of track. Because the land, close to the nation's capital, is so valuable, its redevelopment has been rapid, and virtually no signs of this massive yard are left in 2003.

However, several major yards not owned by the big six railroad companies are still operating. This final chapter of the book is dedicated to describing these yards.

The Bessemer & Lake Erie Railroad had a hump yard in the northern suburbs of Pittsburgh until 1996, when it was downsized and converted to a flat yard. This general view of the yard, taken in 1999, shows three B&LE switchers with a train of iron ore for the local steel mills. The classification bowl occupied the land to the right of the train.

The Blue Island (Indiana Harbor Belt) classification yard, like the one at the other Chicago yard, Clearing (Belt Railroad), exemplify the Chicago melting pot. On May 11, 1995, a Santa Fe transfer arrives at Blue Island as a second train of boxcars is propelled over the hump. Nos. 657 and 3841 arrive with transfer traffic from Corwith, which will be sorted over the hump into one of 44 classification tracks. Blue Island handles 600 cars per shift, with traffic from all the major railroads mixing over the hump.

The yardmaster watches as autoracks are propelled from the pullback tracks at Blue Island. The flat crossing with Ashland Avenue can be seen in the background, as can the Dan Ryan Expressway.

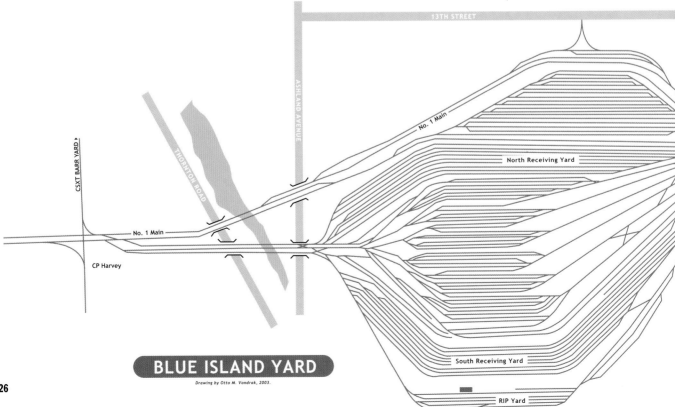

BLUE ISLAND YARD

*Drawing by Otto M. Vondrak, 2003.*

This yard, built by the Indiana Harbor Belt Railroad in 1952, plays a key role in the interchange of cars between the western railroads and Norfolk Southern. Prior to 1998, Conrail was the major user of the facility. The yard lies in southern Chicago, just half a mile south of CSX's Barr Yard. The yard was busy during my visit in 1995, with the hump handling 600 cars per shift.

The yard has 18 receiving tracks, 9 to the north of the bowl and 9 to the south. Hump switching takes place by means of four pullback tracks to the west of the main yard complex. The problem is that they are limited to 40 cars each; any longer rakes of cars need to be pulled back more, fouling the mainline.

The bowl has 44 tracks, the north side of the complex has 19 auxiliary tracks, but the yard has no dedicated departure tracks. Manifest departures are pulled out of the bowl in an easterly direction. Two or three strings of cars are combined in the yard leads to make up a long-distance train.

Three road bridges cross the yard, giving good views of activity. However, this is a fairly rough area of greater Chicago, and during my visit, railroad staff called me onto the property for my own protection. To the west, both the Dan Ryan Expressway and Ashland Avenue cross the hump approach. At the eastern end of the yard, Halstead Street crosses the complex.

The hump at Blue Island as seen from the Dan Ryan Expressway overpass. An Indiana Harbor Belt switcher is propelling its last few cars over the hump.

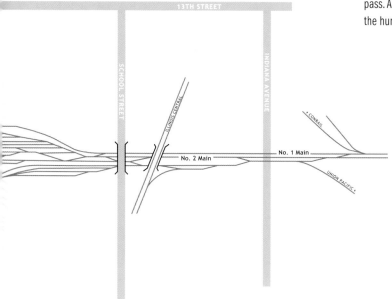

At 5:00 A.M. on a June morning, the new tracks of the rebuilt Kirk Yard are seen from the hump as a pair of EJ&E switchers trims the bowl tracks.

K irk Yard, built in 1952 at a cost of $4.9 million, serves three major steelworks. Previously, it had a 58-track classification bowl and contained 47 miles of track. In 1998, a major rebuild modernized the 1950s hump operation and now provides longer classification tracks.

The yard now has just nine retarders instead of the original 11, and the bowl is divided into 43 tracks, accessed from the hump via the retarders. The 14 longer tracks are no longer used for classification over the hump but handle longer unit trains that run to and from the three local steel mills: U.S. Steel, Inland Steel, and Bethlehem Steel. The yard currently handles 900 cars each day and does most of its interchange work with CSX.

The yard can be found by taking the Gary Steel Mill exit from I-90, then a left turn on what quickly becomes a dirt road along the southern edge of the yard complex. However, this is private property, and it is best to ask permission before driving beyond the engine stabling point.

Looking east from Clearing Yard's modern hump tower, which spans the tracks of both yards, two Belt Railroad GP38-2s fill the air with smoke as they drag cars from the 56-track eastbound bowl for reclassification. On the left are the four 120-car roads leading to the westbound hump, empty except for another pair of BRC GP38-2s ready to pick up more cars from the reception yard, which is in the distance at the upper left corner.

Although Belt Railroad of Chicago owns the massive Clearing Yard, this yard is an integral part of all the major Class 1s. In 1879, the Chicago & Western Indiana Railroad teamed up with the Chicago Great Western to build the Clearing Yard, eventually finishing in 1902. Although these two roads eventually went the way of MoPac and then UP, Belt Railroad was Clearing's owner in 1912. Belt, in turn, was owned by 12 railroad companies, including the Santa Fe and Burlington Railroads.

Clearing was rebuilt in 1912 and was the largest in the world. It survived many challenges and is still owned by the Belt Railroad, which in 1980 had just 10 stakeholders, including BN and ATSF. The other railroads derive from Chesapeake & Ohio, Conrail, Grand Trunk Western, Illinois Central, Louisville & Nashville, Missouri Pacific, Norfolk & Western, and Soo. This basically means that by 2000, every major road had an interest in Clearing Yard: Burlington Northern Santa Fe, UP, Norfolk Southern, CSX, Canadian National, and Canadian Pacific.

The yard received a major rebuild in 1937 and 1938, mainly to allow longer trains to use the yard and to facilitate classification by introducing retarders in the yards. To allow long trains to use the yard, the four tracks from the reception yard to the hump were lengthened from 70 cars to 110 cars. Any heavy manifests with more than 70 cars were spaced out in their arrival times to make sure that the four long roads could accommodate them.

Classification tracks were extended by reducing the number of roads from 54 in each yard to 36 in the westbound yard and 44 in the eastbound. They were restored to 56 in the eastbound yard in 1952 and remain at 36 and 56, respectively, to this day. Plans to abolish the departure yards altogether and allow trains to depart directly from the classification bowls never materialized, so the departure yards also remain.

The 1980s were a difficult time for Clearing, which saw stiff competition for Chicago interchange traffic with Blue Island Yard on the Indiana Harbor Belt (owned by Conrail). By the end of 1989, throughput at Clearing had plummeted from 2,000 cars per day at the start of the decade to just 200 per day. Gradually, they won back traffic, with ATSF returning its interchange trains in 1992. By 1995, the yard was humping 3,000 cars each day and once again switching over 150 industries around the greater Chicago area—back from the brink indeed!

The yard has an eastbound classification system, with 22 reception roads, a 56-track classification bowl, and 25 departure tracks. The westbound system is smaller, with 15 reception roads, 36 classification tracks, and 20 departure roads. The systems lie side by side, such that the humps are adjacent to each other and pass under a common control center. Clearing Yard is still one of the busiest carload facilities in the United States and a great place to watch trains.

Access to the site is not easy, but there are a couple of good places to watch the action. Overpasses cross both the eastern end of the yard (Route 50, Cicero) and the western end (Harlem Street). In addition to this, some access to the main hump is available from 65th and Central. By turning left into Central when traveling west along 65th, you can get some view of the engine servicing point and the main hump tower.

A good place to stay in the neighborhood is the Holiday Inn on Cicero, near Midway Airport—not least because many crews from Clearing overnight here and are good sources of railway gossip and information.

The westbound yard at Clearing is smaller than its eastbound counterpart. Cars are seen descending the hump early one morning in 1995, just after a two-hour break in classification to allow some running repairs to the primary retarder. The five long arrival lines for the eastbound yard (enlarged from their original four in 1952) contain one long arrival from the west. The works truck in the foreground contains not only a winch but welders who will shortly be employed on the primary retarder.

# Sample Departures List for Clearing Yard in May 1995

| TIME | TO | CALLING AT/BLOCKS TO |
|------|-----|----------------------|
| **EAST OF HUMP** | | |
| 00.15 | Neff (UP) | Dolton, Little Rock, St. Louis |
| 01.00 | Croxton, New Jersey (CR) | |
| 04.00 | Blue Island Yard (IHB) | |
| 05.30 | Willard (CSX) | Grand Rapids, Cincinnati, Cumberland |
| 07.00 | Landers Yard (NS) | |
| 07.00 | South Chicago Yard (BRC) | |
| 08.30 | Selkirk (CR) | |
| 11.30 | Bellevue (NS) | |
| 11.59 | Barr Yard (CSX) | |
| 12.30 | Conway Yard (CR) | |
| 14.00 | Toronto (GTW) | Montreal, Flint, Sarina |
| 16.00 | Flat Rock (GTW) | Battle Creek, Sarina |
| 19.00 | Glen Yard (BRC) | |
| 21.00 | Bedford Park Yard (CSX) | |
| 21.00 | Waycross (CSX) | Danville, Nashville, Evansville, Louisville |
| 21.00 | Macon (NS) | Fort Wayne, Knoxville, Chattanooga |
| 21.45 | Elkhart (CR) | |
| | | |
| **WEST OF HUMP** | | |
| 03.30 | Vancouver (CN) | CN intermodal |
| 03.30 | Pine Bluff (SP) | Bloomington, East St. Louis, Eagle Pass |
| 09.00 | Bensenville (CP) | |
| 09.00 | Kansas City (SP) | |
| 09.00 | Roper (SP) | Pueblo |
| 10.00 | St. Paul (CP) | Milwaukee |
| 11.00 | Chicago Central (CC) | |
| 11.00 | Galesburg (BN) | |
| 12.00 | Vancouver (CN) | Thunder Bay, BC Rail |
| 13.30 | Northtown (BN) | |
| 14.00 | Cicero (BN) | Eola |
| 15.00 | Neenah (WC) | Waukesha |
| 16.00 | Calumet (WC) | |
| 20.00 | Proviso (C&NW) | |

The Clearing engine house is something of a United Nations when it comes to road power. This view in 1995 shows BRC Alcos alongside engines from SP, Chessie, GTW, and CN.

The modern hump tower at Clearing spans the hump crest for both east-bound and westbound yards. Here, yardmaster "Pipes" keeps an eye on his screens as he prepares for an eastbound arrival to hump. The east-bound classification tracks can be seen in the background above the yardmaster's head.

The early morning work crew tightens some bolts on Clearing's primary westbound yard retarder in May 1995. Sometimes the staffs at major yards are very welcoming, particularly early in the morning (as here) or late at night.

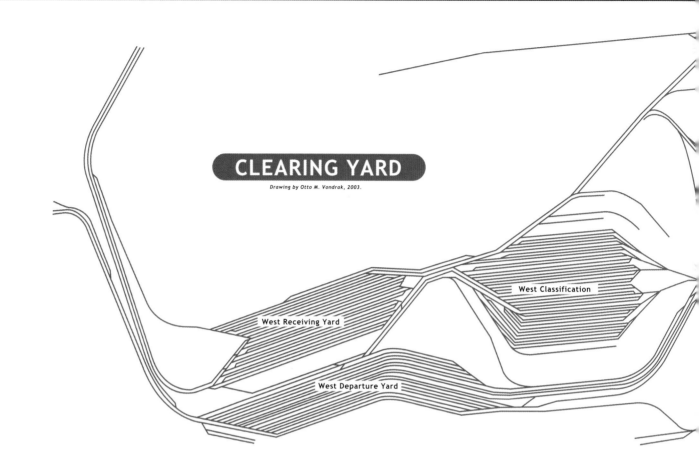

## CLEARING YARD

*Drawing by Otto M. Vondrak, 2003.*

West Classification

West Receiving Yard

West Departure Yard

# TERMINAL RAILROAD ASSOCIATION OF ST. LOUIS

The Broadway Bridge is a good spot to watch arrivals and departures as well as hump switching at Madison Yard. Here, three TRRA switchers push cars over the hump in July 1999.

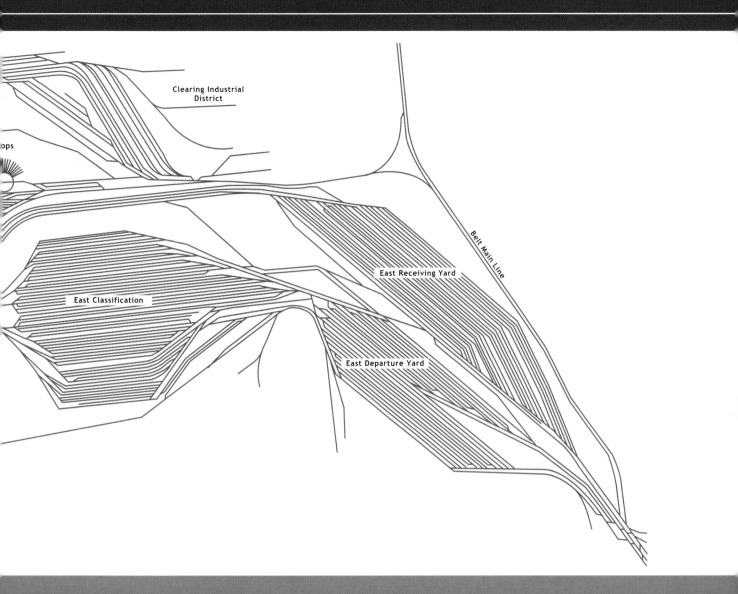

Clearing Industrial
District

ops

Belt Main Line

East Receiving Yard

East Classification

East Departure Yard

# Madison Yard—East St. Louis, Missouri

The Terminal Railroad Association of St. Louis (TRRA), which owns Madison Yard, is in turn owned by five railroads: Burlington Northern Santa Fe, CSX, Norfolk Southern, Illinois Central, and Union Pacific. The facility is the result of a 1974 rebuild that combined four smaller yards in the area. The 11 arrival tracks, 40 classification tracks, and 25 departure roads are laid out parallel to one another. Hump shunting is via a pullout line. Long trains unfortunately do snarl up the mainline, which explains in part why throughput at the yard is small, at 900 cars per day in 1999.

Unlike Gateway, the other hump yard in East St. Louis, access to view Madison Yard is excellent. Crossing over the McKinley Bridge from St. Louis, continue on Broadway, which spans the north end of the yard on an overpass.

## BOOKS

Alexander, E. P. *The Pennsylvania Railroad: A Pictorial History.* New York: Bonanza Books, 1967.

Allen, G. F. *North American Railroads Today.* London: Brian Todd, 1990.

Del Grosso, R. *BNSF 1992 Annual.* Burlington Northern Santa Fe, 1992.

Drury, G. H. and B. Hayden, ed. *Train-Watcher's Guide to North American Railroads, 2nd Ed.* Waukesha, Wisc.: Kalmbach Publishing, 1995.

EuDaly, K. *Argentine in Santa Fe Rails, Vol. 1.* Bucklin, Mo.: White River Productions, 1996.

Hartley, S. *Conrail, Vol. 2: 1983–1990.* Piscataway, N.J.: Railpace Company, Inc., 1990.

Lindsey, S. *Norfolk Southern, 1995 Review.* Mukilteo, Wash.: Hundman, 1995.

Messer, D. W. *Triumph 2: Philadelphia to Harrisburg.* Baltimore, Md.: Barnard Roberts & Co., 1999.

Middleton, W. D. *Landmarks on the Iron Road.* Bloomington, Ind.: Indiana University Press, 1999.

Rhodes, M. *The Illustrated History of British Marshalling Yards.* Hersham, Surrey, U.K.: Oxford Publishing Company [Ian Allen Publishing, Ltd.], 1988.

Roberts, C. S. *Triumph 1: Altoona to Pitcairn.* Baltimore, Md.: Barnard Roberts & Co., 1997.

Roberts, E. W. and D. P. Stremes. *Canadian Trackside Guide 1995.* Ottawa, Ontario: Bytown Railway Society, 1995.

Schafer, M. and B. Solomon. *Pennsylvania Railroad.* Osceola Wisc.: Motorbooks International, 1997.

Solomon, B. and M. Schafer. *New York Central Railroad.* Osecola, Wisc.: Motorbooks International, 1999.

Taylor, J. *Conrail Commodities.* Telford Pa.: Silver Brook Junction Publishing, 1994.

Taylor, J. A. *A Sampling of the Penn Central.* Bloomington, Ind.: Indiana University Press, 1973.

Turner, C. W. et al. *Chessie's Road.* Richmand, Va.: Garret & Massie, 1997.

## OTHER

"Belt Railway Rebuilds Clearing Classification Yard." *Railway Age* July 1938.

Blaszak, M. W. "Illinois Central: Railroad for the Nineties." *TRAINS Magazine* August 1992: 32–40.

———. "Belt Railway of Chicago: Back from the Brink." *TRAINS Magazine* July 1993: 46–53.

Cameron, G. "Conrail's 'Matron on the Ohio.'" *Inside Track* 2001, 18–22.

"Carving up Conrail." *TRAINS Magazine* June 1997: 25–27.

Conrail publication. "A Visitor's Guide to Elkhart Yard." n.d.

———. "Conrail's Conway Yard—A Visitor's Guide." n.d.

———. "Conrail's Selkirk Yard—A Visitor's Guide." n.d.

Crammer, D. C. "Barstow: Servicing the Power." *RailNews* May 1998: 51–59.

CSX Transportation publication. "Rice Yard, Waycross, Georgia." 1994.

Cupper, D. "The Next Merger Shoe Drops." *TRAINS Magazine* January 1997: 26–27.

Cupper, D. and R. S. McGonigal. "Enola Yard Closes— Who's Next?" *TRAINS Magazine* January 1994: 14–15.

Diasy, D. J. Illinois Central Railroad Society. Personal communication with author, June 1995.

Dolzall, G. W. "The First 38 Miles: The Race Track." *TRAINS Magazine* August 1988: 39–49.

———. "The Steel Triangle." *TRAINS Magazine* September 1988: 42–56.

———. "Day by Day at Argentine and Points East." *TRAINS Magazine* May 1990: 48–60.

Droege, J. A. "Yards and Terminals and Their Operation." *Railroad Gazette* 1906.

"Enola Yard Closes, Who's Next?" *TRAINS Magazine* January 1994: 14–15.

Frailey, F. W. "Look Before You Laugh: Conrail from the Inside Out." *TRAINS Magazine* January 1981: 32–41.

Glischinski, S. "A Tale of Twin Cities." *TRAINS Magazine* October 1986: 26–36.

———. "Showdown at Northtown Yard." *TRAINS Magazine* June 2000: 18–21.

Graham-White, S. "The Belt's Clearing Yard." *Pacific Rail News* April 1996: 28–37.

Keefe, K. P. "Pocahontas Pride." *TRAINS Magazine* September 1994: 33–43.

Kelly, B. "Fall of the High Line." *TRAINS Magazine* June 1987: 24–33.

———. "1st Sub Forever." *TRAINS Magazine* July 1987: 22–33.

Knutson, R. and K. Rasmussen. "Dispatching BN's Dakota Division." *TRAINS Magazine* October 1982: 67–71.

Miller, H. L. "Everything's Up to Date in Kansas City." *TRAINS Magazine* June 2000: 40–45.

Murray, T. "World's Best: Worst to First in 10 Years." *TRAINS Magazine* November 2002: 32–45.

Nemeth, T. "Railfanning Allentown-Bethlehem." *Railpace News Magazine* August 1985: 19–27.

Overbey, D. and P. D. Hiatte. "24 Hours at the Crossroads of Frisco." *TRAINS Magazine* January 1981: 22–30.

Penn Central publication. "Penn Central Transportation Company Columbus Yard." n.d.

Pinkepank, J. A. "A Railroad's Railroad." *TRAINS Magazine* September 1966: 36–46.

Santa Fe Railroad publication. *Barstow: Santa Fe's Modern Oasis.* 1971.

Schermerhorn, G. R. "Selkirk! Railfanning Conrail's Big Yard Near Albany, New York." *Railfan & Railroad* April 1997: 39–45.

———. "New York State's Capital Region." *RailNews* May 1998: 35–43.

Stephens, B. "Locomotive Artery." *TRAINS Magazine* January 1996: 43–55.

———. "Hot Times on Norfolk Southern's Nickel Plate Line." *TRAINS Magazine* October 1997: 38–48.

———. "Enola Yard Comes Back, Improving NS Operations." *TRAINS Magazine* April 2002: 13.

"Trackside in Cincinnati." *TRAINS Magazine* September 2002: supplement 1–16.

Truscott, T. and D. Barrett. "Selkirk Super Facts." Mohawk & Hudson Chapter National Railway Historical Society. www.family.knick.net/railroad/se_2.htm

Waite, T. "Hump Yards and Their Evolution." *Mainline Modeller* September 1991: 34-37.

Wrinn, J. "Atlanta: Railroad Capital of the New South." *TRAINS Magazine* July 1994: 32–40.

# INDEX